In A Word

The ABCs of Warmth and Wisdom

In A Word

The ABCs of Warmth and Wisdom

by Carol L. Clark, Ph.D.

BONNEVILLE BOOKS™
SPRINGVILLE, UTAH

ISBN: 1-55517-640-2
e.1

Published by Bonneville Books
Imprint of Cedar Fort Inc.
www.cedarfort.com

Distributed by:

Typeset by Kristin Nelson
Cover design by Nicole Cunningham
Cover design © 2003 by Lyle Mortimer

Printed in the United States of America
10 9 8 7 6 5 4 3 2 1

Printed on acid-free paper

Library of Congress Cataloging-in-Publication Data

Clark, Carol, 1948-
  In a word: the ABCs of warmth and wisdom / by Carol L. Clark.
     p. cm.
  ISBN 1-55517-640-2 (pbk. : alk. paper)
  1. Christian life--Mormon authors. 2. Church of Jesus Christ of
Latter-day Saints--Doctrines. I. Title.

ACKNOWLEDGMENTS

My endless thanks to my beloved brother, Stanford John Clark, for his fine literacy counsel, careful editing, and enduring encouragement.

Many thanks and much love also to MarJean Clark Wilcox and Anne Clark Pingree--loyal cousins, affirming friends, and gentle readers.

Great love and thanks to Marjorie Spencer, my sister by affection, for insights and wisdom that always make things better.

PREFACE

"How forcible are right words!" Job stated passionately to his friends (Job 6:25).

Reading Job recalled to me how true his statement is. Right words—and all they mean—applied to daily life are a true source of strength, direction, and support no matter what others may say.

In a very real sense this alphabet of gospel principles is a capturing of adventures and experiments upon many of the gospel's right words. My prayer is that what I share here will lead every reader to Him who is the Word (John 1:1).

TABLE OF CONTENTS

A IS FOR ANCHORED

One Thanksgiving holiday, I accompanied my mother on a trip to the Antarctic peninsula. On what promised to be a most fascinating day of exploring, our ship dropped anchor in a makeshift harbor in the caldera of a volcano that had been a refuge for whalers during the last century. Whale bones and pieces of crude rendering equipment lined the scant shoreline.

Our daily schedule called for a swim in the thermal waters of this still active volcano, but by 10:00 a.m. when we were to head ashore, the weather had dramatically changed. Weather charts by the purser's office showed the shift of three hurricanes that had been brooding off Cape Horn the day before. Heading suddenly south, these giant storms blew only a few miles from us. They spewed rain that froze before it splattered against our windows and decks, and spawned winds that whipped the ship and all its rigging. Within minutes from the general announcement that the deadly trio bore down upon us, the ship groaned and pitched fiercely as the rain and winds intensified under a glowering sky.

The lowering gray skies turned black, and the crew sank more anchors. Still, the fierceness of the hurricanes required that every hour or so the crew rev the engines and with effort shift the ship. Although well anchored, we drifted inexorably towards the rocks.

Amidst the plummeting of the ship, the staccato of pelting ice, and the whine of that ferocious wind, I sat in a deserted lounge studying the sky, water, and rocks. For as many hours as my increasingly seasick stomach could tolerate, I sat awe-struck, for never before had I encountered such raw weather and such forbidding circumstances.

When the day began, the announcement that the volcano in which we sat had not erupted for twenty years seemed a novel fact. As I experienced the storm, I found myself thinking that the short span of twenty years was about a century short of comforting me. Waves bashed the ship, rains hammered it, and I feared that even the water underneath us could boil to life.

Under me, beside me, over me, nature rolled and fumed hour after hour. Inside me, my physical and, increasingly, my emotional selves churned in concert with the storm. I felt so terribly human—I was not in control, and I was very afraid. I was keenly aware that I was quite literally at the ends of the earth, days from help, a speck on a mammoth ocean in the path of devouring storms.

I can't describe all I felt at being so close to some of the fiercest of the Lord's creations acting on their own terms. That weather and that place of stark ice, black water, bare rock and bleak sky rained and reigned. Humbled, intrigued, and frightened, I silently watched and prayed. The storm raged long before I gave in to my uncomfortable stomach and had to lie down. As the ship groaned and bobbed for hours more, I lay quietly in my bunk, physically unwell and quite overcome with all I felt.

I prayed from the core of my being to the Lord of all, knowing He was master of those hurricanes too. I prayed as one lost and alone, for I surely was both.

At some point during that long vigil, my feelings centered on a new, welcome emotion. Even as the ship plunged and lurched, the deep fear I experienced ebbed away. My great internal storm grew calm, and I nestled into that eye of peace while the giant storms churned on around me. Far from the end of that trial, I began to feel wrapped in a mantle of supreme comfort. Despite my anxiety and the foment of the weather and my physical self, I knew all would be well. I knew not how or when, but with certainty, I knew all was well, all was well.

Often in subsequent days, after the hurricanes had roared past, I sought quiet refuge in front of the same lounge window through which I'd studied some of the glories of our Heavenly Father's creations during a mighty storm. I read the scriptural creation stories as the icebergs drifted by. Still humbled and intrigued, I pondered what it means to fear the Lord, and I silently prayed my thanks.

That hiatus from all I knew in my normal life taught me much about the peace that passeth understanding.

Paul admonished:

> Be careful for nothing; but in every thing by prayer and supplication with thanksgiving let your requests be made known unto God.
>
> And the peace of God, which passeth all understanding, shall keep your hearts and minds through Christ Jesus (Philippians 4:6-7).

The blessings of peace endured even after the storm dissipated, and even when we rejoined the world. I learned that in the midst of even the fiercest storms, we may be tried, but we don't have to be terrified. We will be challenged, but we don't have to be vanquished, for we can be anchored with the peace of God that "passeth all understanding."

On that Thanksgiving, I gave thanksgiving for my basic safety and for the resultant peace that vanquished my internal storm and anchored my soul, even while the elements warred.

B IS FOR BELONGING

When I planned for a whirlwind tour of Australia, I knew it must be a carry-on affair. I had been assigned to be a junior companion on a training trip throughout the entire Australian continent. I had three plane connections en route to Sydney, and the three weeks I'd spend on that continent would be a series of speaking assignments interspersed with airports. Carry-on was the only way to take my belongings.

My traveling companion and I discussed at length what we'd take and how we'd carry it. I shopped accordingly, buying new clothes, shoes and accessories for this unique occasion. At our first plane connection, I wondered, as I dragged my luggage from the beginning of one concourse to the end of another, if I had brought too much. I mentally went through my packing list while I trudged along. No, I concluded, as I readjusted the shoulder straps, I had brought enough clothes and materials to get the job done. I could go the distance, luggage and all.

Our arrival in Sydney thrilled me. I anxiously urged my unwieldy bags down the airplane aisle as we deplaned. I bumped and caught on seats and armrests in my rush. What an adventure lay ahead!

The men greeting us took the bags, and I welcomed the reprieve. In a flurry of hellos and briefings, they piled the bags in the back, put us in the front of a four-wheel type vehicle, then whisked us downtown for a lunch overlooking Sydney Harbor.

After a tasty meal and introduction to our work, we arrived at the Area Presidency Offices to get ready for our first meeting. The brethren opened the "boot" of the car to bring out our luggage. All the happy chatter stopped abruptly when they discovered that while my companion's bags were still there, mine were not. They couldn't believe it, and I was in shock. All of us looked in the boot, under the seats, on the ground. My luggage was missing, all right. All of it.

One of the men checked the windows. "Look at this," he cried. "Someone broke the latch, slid the back window open and grabbed all the bags he could reach— yours, Sister Clark." He dashed off to call the car park security office.

A scant two hours before the start of our first training session, I had only the shirt on my back. No scriptures. No notes. No fresh clothes. No change of shoes. No glasses. Not even a lipstick. I quickly canceled credit cards before our wonderful hostess scurried with me to a local mall. I prayed the entire way that I would be able to find toiletries and something to wear. I grabbed a toothbrush and some cosmetics, and settled for the first outfit that fit, regardless of style and price.

Upon our return, I foraged through my companion's notes, borrowed some scriptures, grabbed my prescription sunglasses, which, fortunately, I'd been wearing when we went to lunch, and dashed to the training.

As I stood at the pulpit wearing my glasses, I felt about as dreary as that room looked through the darkened lenses. I also felt foolish. What was going to be three carefully planned weeks out of a suitcase had become three weeks out of a purse. And I didn't even have a purse!

I began my talk by explaining why I was wearing my very dark glasses. A huge "Oh no!" rose from the audience. After the meeting, women streamed up, apologizing profusely that such a terrible thing would happen to a visitor to their country. "Maybe the thief will benefit from your scriptures," one said. I smiled at such kindness and concern. These good people cheered me and provided much-needed perspective.

The next day I borrowed a large purse, folded my few possessions into it and off we went. Those next few days we traveled from city to city. Each morning I'd awake and ask my friend, "Hmm, what shall I wear today?" Each evening, I'd experience something wonderful at the hands of the Australians.

The Sydney Saints had called ahead. From sister to brother, from friend to friend, from mother to daughter, in city after city, the Saints let others know that Sister Clark had no clothes. I didn't set foot in one building that some sister didn't come forward and quietly press a pair of hose or a note into my hand. With a pat and a loving word, these women welcomed me. Even more important, their gestures and small gifts made me feel I belonged—sunglasses, wrinkled clothes and all.

I saw as I might not have under any other circumstances, that what mattered was not *belongings,* but *belonging.* To have those women I did not know do so much to comfort, help and welcome me wrapped me in a warmth I'd never have duplicated with anything out of my long lost suitcases.

Belongings are good, but *belonging* is better. That's what those Australian sisters taught me. Alma the Elder taught his people, by way of commandment, "that . . . they should look forward with one eye, having one faith and one baptism, having their hearts knit together in unity and in love one towards another" (Mosiah 18:21). To be knit together in love means, in part, to belong to each other, to belong together. Like yarns woven to make a garment, the threads of loving concern provide a covering as real as any fabric, a mantle that never goes out of style, loses its fit, or fails to wear well.

Belonging didn't diminish the loss of my luggage in a physical sense. But in a spiritual sense, the Australian sisters clothed me in some finery I'd never worn before. I saw how thoroughly charitable acts prove to be a most durable mantle. When I joked with my new-found friends about three weeks out of a purse, when they sympathized with me, when they rallied to do little things to help me, I felt I belonged with them, that they belonged to me, no matter how I looked. When I felt I belonged, two suitcases of belongings didn't seem nearly so important.

I left Australia carrying a small cardboard box of little more than a dozen pairs of hose and one skirt. The security officers at the car park never found a trace of my luggage, and I have no idea if the thief profited from my scriptures or not. I do know how much I gained from my loss.

Being "knit together," as Alma phrased it, for me had little to do with the same old shirt I'd worn for days and everything to do with the small gestures that together represented cases full of kindness. I'd fussed over my belongings all the way to Australia. I returned home rejoicing that I'd been taught so much about belonging.

C IS FOR CHARITY

If anyone were to ask me what was the most important lesson I've learned in the last five years, I'd answer without hesitation, "Charity Never Faileth." The Lord taught, "And above all things, clothe yourself with the bond of charity, as with a mantle, which is the bond of perfectness and peace" (D&C 88:125). After his great discourse about prayer, Amulek taught:

> . . . if ye turn away the needy, and the naked, and visit not the sick and afflicted, and impart of your substance, if ye have, to those who stand in need—I say unto you, if ye do not any of these things, behold, your prayer is vain, and availeth you nothing, and ye are as hypocrites who do deny the faith.
>
> Therefore, if ye do not remember to be charitable, ye are as dross, which the refiners do cast out, (it being of no worth) and is trodden under foot of men.
>
> . . . I would that ye would come forth and harden not your hearts any longer . . . (Alma 34:28-29, 31).

We recognize charity in myriad ways, among them:

The way we feel (The "word of the Lord came to [Mormon] by the power of the Holy Ghost, saying: . . . I am filled with charity, which is everlasting love" Moroni 8:7, 17).

What we do ("relieve the oppressed" Isaiah 1:17).

9

How we do it ("Let all your things be done with charity" Corinthians 16:14).

Actually, this bit of scripture I've shared is but a small sample of all that exists on the subject of charity. Yet, what's here tells us so clearly that charity is in some ways like a great crossroads. Those who seek the pathway of charity can be clearly recognized, as can those who go in the opposite direction.

I remember an occasion when I attended a bridal shower. I knew the mother of the bride, and that was about it. I sat on the periphery of the conversation because I'd come late, straight from another appointment. I waved at my friend Susan, introduced myself to the women on either side, and tried hard to think of what to say next.

Just then, the hostess emerged from the kitchen. She invited everyone to the dining room table and came straight over to me. She welcomed me, introduced herself, then did something quite extraordinary. She looked me right in the eye and said, "Thank you for being Susan's friend."

The words weren't unusual, but the way she said them drew me in. This was far from ordinary chit chat. This was a rare personal acknowledgment, spoken with such kindness and generosity that I felt the message, not just heard it. I have not forgotten the feeling I had as that charitable woman spoke those few words.

I believe that charity is often that simple and that salient. In thousands of ways, it quietly and clearly blesses the world one person at a time.

When I was a girl, I thought charity and casseroles were synonymous. My dear mother delivered endless casseroles and other culinary delights to funerals, ward dinners, ailing neighbors, new mothers, as well as to the weary and aged.

In my teenage years, I began to think of charity and puberty as close associates. I believed that, like my wonderful mom, I'd become charitable and willingly serve, care for others' children, help my family, and do all the other fine things I watched my mother do, when I grew into womanhood and had my own kitchen.

It has been in my adult years that I've learned that my youthful notions were both right and wrong. While casseroles are not charity, in the creations borne of our hearts and hands, we demonstrate charity. The onset of puberty does not necessarily signal the development of charity, but no matter what our age or culinary abilities, we can be exceedingly charitable.

I think of a Church party I attended recently in which I watched charity play its loving hand. A nine year-old girl was helping her six year-old cousin learn how to play tic-tac-toe. I know what a competitor this girl is because I've played games with her before. She patiently kept explaining the game to her cousin, letting him win over and over, something she never lets me do.

In another corner of the room, the Young Women president spotted a Laurel who didn't attend Church all the time. The leader stopped what she was doing and went right over to that girl. They were soon laughing and joking together.

A home teacher and his family had brought an elderly widow to the party. Very deaf and too proud to wear a hearing aid, she asked, "What?" after each sentence spoken by family members. Finally, the home teacher changed places with his son and sat right by this sister, repeating the conversation so she could understand everything.

The bishop and his wife, both naturally shy people, moved from table to table, greeting everyone. A Relief Society committee tutored the deacons in the fine art of serving food. The Primary chorister accompanied the Mia Maids when they sang a song.

So it went. In a hundred small ways, a ward wore charity as a mantle.

I know of a man who encountered a particularly difficult situation at work that required he draw that mantle close around him. Matt, my friend, had been recruited by a man who held high ecclesiastical position in Matt's ward to join the homebuilding firm this man and his nephew owned. My friend had been hired to put structure to the business practices and to be sure they were in compliance with the law.

It wasn't long before Matt discovered that the uncle and nephew were woefully out of compliance and that their daily business practices lacked ethics. He followed his conscience and his contractual obligations and raised these issues with his boss. The boss squirmed but did nothing.

Months went on. The two owners, by now very unhappy with these regular reminders of their own behavior, began to reap the fruits of their harvest. Business dropped off precipitously, and the twosome, blaming senior management, let people go.

In the middle of this firing frenzy, Matt got caught. The owners demanded that he let another senior employee go, an employee the two particularly disliked because he too had raised ethical issues about business practices.

Uncle and nephew demanded that Matt fire the man after enumerating to him all his shortcomings and reading him a full-blown riot act. Matt responded, "It's bad enough that he'll lose his job. What merit is there in telling him all his faults? If you have found fault with him, you may want to tell him yourselves. For me to do it lacks charity, and I cannot in good conscience deliver that message."

The nephew exploded, "Well, then we'll just have to let you go too." Matt's ecclesiastical leader lowered his head and said nothing as Matt walked out.

Matt faced a grave dilemma. He had grounds to file a lawsuit and a complaint with the government. He felt angry and hurt, plus he faced the daunting task of looking for other employment. He struggled to decide what the best course of action was.

After much soul-searching in the temple and many quiet hours of contemplation and prayer, he came to a conclusion. He'd lost his job over an issue of charity; he'd maintain his integrity by acting with charity. He read over and over the scriptures about charity, including this one:

"And charity suffereth long, and is kind, and envieth not, and is not puffed up, seeketh not her own, is not easily provoked, thinketh no evil, and rejoiceth not in iniquity but rejoiceth in the truth, beareth all things, believeth all things, hopeth all things, endureth all things" (Moroni 7:45).

He took strength from knowing that "if ye have not charity, ye are nothing, for charity never faileth" (Moroni 7:46). He knew well charity is not a doormat doctrine. By being charitable, he was not waiting to be kicked again. Rather, he felt called to work towards resolution with long-suffering and kindness.

He knew that charity is a spiritual gift, requiring that he "pray unto the Father with all the energy of heart" (Moroni 7:48). At his moment of extremity, praying in such a fashion required that he dig deep within his own spiritual resources. He knew he must trust the Lord and act out his faith that "charity never faileth" even when his livelihood and reputation were on the line, and dishonorable behaviors seemed to bear sway.

The circumstances required months of charitable effort on Matt's part. After all was said and done, Matt could testify to the significance of the doctrine of charity. When he encountered his two former bosses in a Church meeting some months later, he could look both in the eye without qualm, and that was a sweet proof to him that charity never faileth.

At home, charity is in constant demand. We sorely need it so we refrain from saying and doing the harmful while we relish each opportunity to respond with kindness. Most of all, we need that pervasive love and kindness that exemplify charity. We need to know that due to this great spiritual gift, we can respond in ways that build, not burn bridges. We can see and be more. We can enrich the lives of others as we provide for them in ways otherwise unattainable. Like Matt, in moments of great crisis and calm, we can lean on the Lord, following the prophets' counsel and knowing that charity is the ever-steady, ever-ready love of our Savior.

Charity, "the pure love of Christ," endures. Past the stereotypes, in great ways and small, in the office and at home, with colleagues and confidantes, "Charity Never Faileth."

D is for Demonstrate

Without equivocation, I say that those who demonstrate their understanding of charity are a rare breed. Truly rare. When I find those wonderful people, I follow them around, if I can, and ask questions and observe. I've heard lots of nice talks about charity, and I have learned from them. But it's not the talkers, it's the doers I pursue.

One of the most valuable lessons I've learned from them is that treating people in charitable ways is an act of will, a demonstration of spiritual understanding and discipline. It's a way of showing that we have become adults in a spiritual, mental, emotional sense. Treating people in charitable ways is also a demonstration of faith.

Knowing I state the obvious, I still say it is not always easy to demonstrate charity and kindness for others. One reason is that we will not always get our own way if we practice charity. We will not always be the boss, even if we hold the title. We will not always be the center of attention, even if we hold center stage. Of course, all of that is because we are thinking of others as well as ourselves.

And as every parent and leader knows, looking out for the good of others as well as one's self is usually a thankless job. I personally do not know of any teenagers who have run to their mothers and fathers saying, "Oh, thank you for saving me from myself," when a parent has curtailed some activity, enforced a curfew or held onto the car keys. It seems that only maturity and life experience may bring the insight that those who set and enforce rules are usually those who love us the most.

Charity is such a demonstration of spiritual discipline and depth. It requires of us that we think, feel, and act with a perspective borne of love of the Lord and love of others, which can, in some circumstances, require great spiritual effort. The point is that the charitable are cognizant of their own ambitions and needs, but they are motivated by something beyond them.

As a school teacher, I was often distressed that some of my students lacked the ability to sit still or to learn basic material. I attributed much of their behavior to their youth. In more recent years, I've thought that another major reason that some of those high schoolers learned so little was that they lacked desire and discipline. "You gotta wanna," I'd tell my students, knowing even desire was insufficient for the need. "Then you gotta do," I would add. I always knew when a high school sophomore was close to getting a driver's license. That was the quarter when the student's language shifted from "I want a B" to "I've got to get a B." And behavior followed.

I have often thought about Mormon's admonition that we "pray unto the Father with all the energy of heart, that ye [we] may be filled with this love [charity], which he hath bestowed upon all who are true followers of his Son, Jesus Christ . . ." (Moroni 7:48). Some significant spiritual work begins when we reach the point that we feel we have "got to" be blessed with charity. A demonstration of faith precedes the gift itself.

The Bible Dictionary explains, "The object of prayer is not to change the will of God, but to secure for ourselves and for others blessings that God is already willing to grant, but that are made conditional on our asking for them. Blessings require some work or effort on our part before we can obtain them. Prayer is a form of work, and is an appointed means for obtaining the highest of all blessings" (Bible Dictionary, p. 753). Whenever I read this statement, I realize that, like some of my former students, I must realize that the onus is on me to demonstrate my earnestness. What is true of prayer is true of all other spiritual skills—they require practice and work, i.e., that we demonstrate our desire to achieve them.

Demonstrating charity requires "all the energy of heart," which is a measure of its spiritual importance. I am blessed to have a distant cousin who has given that energy of heart to her own pursuit of charity. During a season of some loss for me, I wrote her a letter about my woes. From literally halfway around the world, she got up at 2 A.M. to call me. Unfortunately, I had gone out for a very early morning walk, and I missed the call. This dear cousin left me a message that I saved and played and replayed.

Even ten thousand miles away, over a crackling telephone line, even though some of the words were garbled by bad wiring, I got the message. Her loving counsel documented to me that her own demonstrations of faith and works had resulted in deep insights about how charity is won and wielded. That message represented far more than words, it demonstrated my cousin's commitment to charity and her hard work to earn it.

My cousin and all those have paid the price for charity demonstrate the Lord's love for us each time they bless others. How rare and fine are such demonstrably charitable souls.

E IS FOR EGO

One of the least understood rules of life is the one about checking your ego, along with your coat, at the door. The rule is not stated in scripture the way I've just said it, but it's in the good books just the same.

In the Liberty Jail, Joseph Smith wrote:

> We have learned by sad experience that it is the nature and disposition of almost all men, as soon as they get a little authority, as they suppose, they will immediately begin to exercise unrighteous dominion (D&C 121:39).

My echo to those words is stated in my belief that when people do not check their egos at the door, difficulties result.

Some years ago when I was in my "salad days," as Shakespeare phrased it, "still green in judgment," I often worked with high-powered political, business, education, and community leaders. I discovered during those fascinating forays into serious politics and business that the quest for power and money did not do good things to people. Right before my eyes, on many occasions I watched some otherwise decent men and women become grasping, blood-sucking creatures when they determined to pursue their own interests at any cost.

I not only observed, but was occasionally singed by,

19

these Machiavellian machinations:

- Saying whatever would bring the desired object.
- Stabbing innocents in the back, then stepping over them as if they had disappeared once they'd fallen.
- Betraying trusts.
- Receiving wholehearted loyalty but never returning that precious gift.
- Forgetting that kindness is not optional among those who are true followers of Christ, no matter what the political expediency.
- Receiving so much service that one forgets how to serve.

Such behavior, which abounded and seemed well rewarded, led me to think often about the Prophet Joseph's experiences with those having a "little authority."

During those days among the powerful, I longed deeply to understand the character of people like the Prophet Joseph and King Benjamin, individuals who had truly learned how to check their own egos. I was especially fascinated by King Benjamin, who held great authority but who never lapsed into unrighteous dominion. At the conclusion of many a meeting, I said to myself, "How did King Benjamin do it? He ascended to the height of power, but that rarified throne never became a Rameumptom. Where was his ego while he was king?"

I made it my quest to answer those questions, for King Benjamin's example proved to me that neither position, nor power, nor pound notes can dissuade a true believer. All my seeking led me to these particular insights:

1. King Benjamin had pure motives and knew what he was doing. ". . . I have not commanded you to come up hither to trifle with the words which I shall speak, but that you should hearken unto me, and open your ears that ye may hear, and your hearts that ye may understand, and your minds that the mysteries of God may be unfolded to your view" (Mosiah 2:9).

2. The king never forgot how he got where he was. He understood his relationship to his people and his reliance on the Lord. "I have not commanded you to come up hither that ye should fear me...I have been chosen by this people, and consecrated by my father, and was suffered by the hand of the Lord that I should be a ruler and a king over this people; and have been kept and preserved by his matchless power, to serve you with all the might, mind and strength which the Lord hath granted unto me" (Mosiah 2:10-11).

3. King Benjamin knew who he was. "I . . . myself am . . . a mortal man . . . . I am like as yourselves, subject to all manner of infirmities in body and mind . . ." (Mosiah 2:10-11).

4. However he may have been served, he continued to serve others, knowing, thereby, that he served the Lord. "I, myself, have labored with mine own hands that I might serve you, and that ye should

not be laden with taxes, and that there should nothing come upon you which was grievous to be borne . . . I do not desire to boast, for I have only been in the service of God" (Mosiah 2:14, 16).

When he discussed service, it was not strictly in our human context. Rather, he immediately drew the connection between human interaction and our relationship with the Lord. Service, he taught, connects us one to the other; it also connects us to our God.

5. King Benjamin understood his relationship to others.

I tell you these things that ye may learn wisdom; that ye may learn that when ye are in the service of your fellow beings, ye are only in the service of your God (Mosiah 2:17).

To King Benjamin, the people were not his lackeys, serfs, or subordinates, they were his "fellow beings." That phrase suggests parity and mutual respect to me.

For King Benjamin, the great whole was not exclusively his kingdom. It included his attitudes and actions, how his thoughts and behavior affected others and how his desires and works related to keeping the Lord's commandments.

That was it! The king never operated in a vacuum as if he were the center of the universe. His real world was not political or financial, it was spiritual, and the implications of his actions remained ever clear to him, whatever his position in this life. His energies were not directed at his own ego, but at blessing others. In a very real sense, what checked King Benjamin's ego was his own knowledge of who he was, how he related to the Lord, and how he connected with others.

Such insights helped me piece together some most puzzling and challenging experiences in my own life. They also drew me to the conclusion that checking our egos at the door is necessary if we are ever to preclude turning into bugs, alleviate unrighteous dominion, and avoid many ego-driven ills.

F is for Family

I was on a business trip, alone in Toronto, Canada when my brother called. "Sit down, Carol," he began, and my heart sank. "Dad passed away today. He had a massive heart attack and a couple of hours later, he was gone."

That sudden parting brought a grief as dark and impenetrable as the moonless, starless sky through which I flew home. Staring into the blackness, I felt as bleak as that sky looked. I deplaned in a deserted Calgary Airport at 1 A.M. to wait for an early morning plane. Forlorn and all by myself, I felt a rawness of soul that made breathing painful and sleep impossible.

I searched for comfort in moments of prayer and passages of scripture. I soaked in the Savior's words, "I am the resurrection, and the life" (John 11:25) because I so needed that reassurance. I had a tape of Handel's Messiah with me, and I played repeatedly, "I know that my Redeemer lives . . ."

It was not until I embraced members of my family in the sunlight of the following day that I realized it was my father and mother who had taught me that in my personal prayers and scripture study I could find comfort. And I did feel peace in knowing that the spiritual skills my parents had taught me were precisely what I turned to first when one of them left mortality.

From this and many other experiences of tragedy

and joy, I have learned the importance of families. As a single woman who longs for a good husband and my own children, I perhaps take family relationships more seriously than many people who are so busy dealing with their own families that they scarcely acknowledge the wonder of joining as man and wife to raise little ones and care for big ones. I treasure the richness, challenge and diversity of family relationships through many seasons of life.

I don't expect these relationships to be easy. How could they be when they are such an important and long-lasting training ground? Friends, colleagues and neighbors may come and go, but family relationships endure. We are, after all, sealed in the temple with the potential to become eternal family units, not eternal business partnerships or neighborhoods.

The Lord often teaches us through family settings. Even a cursory look at the scriptures shows that the Lord uses familial relationships as the means to help us understand critical truths, such as who we are and how we are to interact. Consider these few:

- We have Heavenly Parents. We are their literal sons and daughters.

- The Savior is often identified by family names, including the Son of Man (Matt. 9:6) and the only begotten Son (John 1:18). Matthew called his account of the Savior's life, "the book of the generation of Jesus Christ, the son of David, the son of Abraham" (Matt. 1:1).

- Alma the elder explained to his people the fruit of unity and love: "And thus they became the children of God" (Mosiah 18:22).

- James defined "pure religion" in part as "to visit the fatherless and widows in their affliction" (James 1:27).

- Each week at Church we even call each other brother and sister.

Family relationships, even figurative ones, link us inextricably.

In a very real sense, our lineage links us too. Blood is thicker than water. It was my feisty survivor of a grandmother who taught me those words and that idea. (I'll never forget the time she killed the rat in Mrs. Petty's basement with only a broom.) She believed family members have a responsibility to love and care for each other. Despite troubles and differences, to Grandma, family was family. My mother, Grandma Colt's oldest daughter, taught her five children to love each other and to be worthy of our heritage.

With the help of my own much-loved parents, brothers, sister, brother- and sisters-in-law, and some extended family, I've learned much about what family relationships can be at their best, their funniest, their wobbliest, and their worst. I do not claim to understand the myriad of family circumstances in which we Church members find ourselves. But based on my personal experience, I have concluded that doing everything we can to bless each other is the least we can do as family members.

When my dear dad dropped me off at the airport for my trip to Canada, he pulled my suitcase from the trunk of the car. As I took it from him, I gave him a hug and said, "Thanks, Dad. I love you." Those were the last words I spoke to him in mortality.

I hope "I love you," are the words each of my family hears from me every time we're together.

G is for Gratitude

A package of balloons was the last thing I packed before I left on a school-sponsored tour of Russia. I reasoned that since the high school students I was escorting would be in Moscow for what was likely their first Fourth of July away from home, I should bring balloons along in place of firecrackers.

When on the third week of our trip we arrived in Moscow, I rummaged through my bag and pulled out the now crushed packages of sparklers, American flags and balloons. At breakfast on the Fourth, the other teachers and I placed our flags-on-a-toothpick in the ubiquitous plates of brown bread and planned a short celebration as we ate dollops of red caviar served on hard-boiled eggs.

Late in the afternoon we found ourselves in a small Moscow park where we blew up our balloons, waved our flags and sang an unmelodious but lusty version of "The Star-Spangled Banner." Tanya, our twenty-three-year-old Russian tour guide, politely held an American flag in one hand and a pink balloon in the other while we relished our party.

After "Yankee Doodle Dandy" and "You're a Grand Old Flag," we created our fireworks—we jumped on, poked and batted every balloon until it obligingly exploded. As the noise crescendoed, I looked at Tanya. "Come on!" I encouraged, "Pop your balloon."

She looked stricken. "Oh no," she responded immediately. "This is a beautiful pink balloon. I love balloons.
I haven't had a balloon since I was a child. I think I'll
save it." With that she undid the knot, carefully let the
air out, and slid a used pink balloon into her pocket.

The celebration ended; our trip ended. Some weeks
later I stood in the midst of a national political convention on the night the presidential candidate was
nominated. On the right cue, thousands of balloons fell.
Almost instantly up to my waist in them, I watched yet
hundreds more fall while my fellow delegates stomped,
punched and bludgeoned them into noisy acknowledgment of our political process.

I stood quietly, holding one balloon, suddenly trans-
ported back to the Fourth of July in Moscow. Memories
and emotions flooded back to me in that deluge of
balloons. I watched again in my mind's eye something
I'd never imagined—an adult cautiously guarding one,
valued balloon.

The celebration ended; the convention ended. As I
returned home, I thought about what I'd learned from
balloons. In my entire life I'd never thought about them
before. Taken for granted, balloons were tokens at birth-
days and parties, something to add a splash of color and
little else. But they were something to be grateful for too,
I realized from Tanya.

Like so many small, insignificant things and events,
balloons can be an occasion to thank the Lord for the
blessings they represent. We are blessed to live in a time
when such frivolities are so readily available and so inex-
pensive that we have no need to give them more than a
passing thought. What a luxury.

Alma admonished, ". . . when thou risest in the

morning let thy heart be full of thanks unto God . . ."
(Alma 37:37). Jacob counseled, "Behold, my beloved
brethren, remember the words of your God; . . . give
thanks unto his holy name by night. . . ." (2 Nephi 9:52).
For clouds and colors, for food and family, for
plumbing and possessions, for truth and travels, for
vehicles and voting, for breath and something as simple
as a balloon, we can be grateful here and abroad,
morning and night.

H IS FOR HARK

I went to Hong Kong just before Christmas for the major purpose of visiting the temple. My mother, brother, and I wanted to see this grand House of the Lord, but despite considerable effort, we had a hard time getting good directions to it. My contacts could get me as close as the right subway exit. After that, the directions were along the lines of, "Look around and you'll find it."

On our designated temple day, we made our way through the subway just fine. It was upon getting to ground level that we simply did not know where to go. The street was empty of traffic, and all we could see were tall cement walls surrounding every house and building. I stood there listening to silence, a rare sound in Hong Kong and the opposite of the subway racket underground. Not a person was in sight.

How, I wondered, could we find the temple? "Where do we go? Where do we go?" I kept asking myself. I walked to the end of the block and turned a corner. Down several blocks I could see a busy thoroughfare with lots of traffic. Some bicyclists whizzed by, and I looked around, hoping someone might stop. Still puzzled about what to do, I stood still, waiting for another passerby or some insight.

Just then my sharp-eyed brother shouted, "There it is!" On the hill above that busy street, in the distance stood Moroni atop a steeple. It was the temple, bathed at that moment in sun. We looked up and moved on, following that beacon to where we should go.

After a very satisfying session, we took the subway back to Kowloon's bustling business district. Again amidst a panoply of city noises, we made our way to a music store with two drawing points: a wonderful classical music section and a couch. Plopping gratefully on the couch, I said hello to the store clerk, a pleasant young man who spoke superb English. Because we'd been in the store everyday and bought something to "pay" for each rest on the couch, he remembered us. Few people were in the store at that moment, so with the temple still fresh in my mind, I asked the clerk if he'd mind playing some Christmas music for us. We so wanted to celebrate the season just then. Obliging us, he immediately switched to a new CD.

The couch, located directly underneath the huge speakers, rumbled as trumpets began a fanfare. First distant, then closer, the trumpets announced I did not know what. Then a clear soprano began, "Hark! The herald angels sing glory to the newborn king."

For the first time in all the times I'd sung that hymn, I listened to the words. The couch shook in a crescendo:

> Light and life to all he brings,
> Ris'n with healing in his wings.
> Mild he lays his glory by,
> Born that man no more may die;
> Born to raise the sons of earth,
> Born to give them second birth.
> Hark! the herald angels sing
> Glory to the newborn King! (Hymns, 209)

When the trumpets finally faded, I was moved. In my mind's eye I saw again Moroni, a herald angel, who had so recently beckoned me from the top of a sunlit steeple on a Kowloon hilltop. "There it is!" we'd shouted, like lost souls found, and rushed on to where we should go and to the renewal found only in the House of the Lord.

Now, listening on that couch, I pondered what it meant to all of us that he was there, trumpet to his lips, announcing the restoration of the gospel. The Prophet Joseph actually listened to his voice, I thought. And I can hear it too.

On that reverberating couch, quite surrounded by Christmas carols, I reflected on the first word of the Doctrine and Covenants, "Hearken." As this dispensation opened, the Lord called us to hear:

> Hearken, O ye people of my church, saith the voice of him who dwells on high, and whose eyes are upon all men; yea, verily I say: Hearken ye people from afar; and ye that are upon the islands of the sea, listen together.
>
> For verily the voice of the Lord is unto all men, and there is none to escape; and there is no eye that shall not see, neither ear that shall not hear, neither heart that shall not be penetrated (D&C 1:1-2).

As I listened to the universally applicable messages of Christmas, I had heard in a hymn I'd known since girlhood, something new, something that made me hearken. I was at that moment so grateful for Moroni's trumpet-clear message of restoration, for his symbolic, clarion call atop the temples of the world.

Joseph Smith wrote:

> Now, what do we hear in the gospel which we have received? A voice of gladness! A voice of mercy from heaven; and a voice of truth out of the earth; glad tidings for the dead; a voice of gladness for the living and the dead; glad tidings of great joy. How beautiful upon the mountains are the feet of those that bring glad tidings of good things, and that say unto Zion: Behold, thy God reigneth! As the dews of Carmel, so shall the knowledge of God descend upon them!
>
> And again, what do we hear? Glad tidings from Cumorah! Moroni, an angel from heaven, declaring the fulfillment of the prophets—the book to be revealed . . . . (D&C 128:19-20).

I had emerged from a maze of unknowns to follow a herald angel. "Hark!" I raised my eyes to the messenger on the steeple of the temple.

In the House of the Lord I had participated with an international assembly in saving ordinances. "Hark!" I heard as never before.

In a foreign land, on that warm December day, I lifted my voice and heart to sing, "Hark! Glory to the newborn king."

I IS FOR INFLUENCE

Belle Spafford, who served as General President of the Relief Society for twenty-nine years, told this wonderful story:

> I recall at one time when I first served in a Relief Society presidency, the ward had built a new meetinghouse and they had to raise a few thousand dollars more in order to have it dedicated on the date scheduled. Relief Society was called upon to prepare and serve a turkey dinner to a large group. It was the first dinner in the new meetinghouse. We found the kitchen to be insufferably small. The women were in each other's way, slowing up the service. One woman fainted from the heat. The next day, in distress over this circumstance, I went to see the bishop. I explained the situation and requested that they knock out one wall and extend the kitchen to include the adjoining space which had been allocated to a classroom. He responded with sharpness. "'Certainly not,'" he said, "we aren't going to start remodeling this building before it is dedicated," and he summarily dismissed me.
>
> On my way home, discouraged and feeling somewhat reprimanded, I called at the home of one of the older sisters, and I poured forth my troubles. I concluded by saying, "In this church men have all the

power; the women are just helpless." To this she
replied, "Oh, no, my dear, the women are not helpless." Then she added, "If someone came to you, Sister
Spafford, and had a good but different gift in each
hand, and one was power and the other influence and
you had a choice, which gift would you choose?"

I thought of this seriously for a moment and then
I said, "I think I would choose influence."

"You probably did, my dear," she said. "Influence
is a great gift of God to women." Then she said,
"Appreciate it and use it aright. Do not covet that
which has been given to the brethren." This was a
great lesson which I have never forgotten. I commend
it to you young women in your companionships, in
your homes, and in your church and community life
(Belle S. Spafford, "Woman in Today's World," *BYU
Speeches of the Year*, March 3, 1970, p. 5).

I love this story, and I have been blessed by it.
Influence, as Sister Spafford suggested, is a much under-
rated tool that allows the user to work wonders. It seems
to me that Ammon used influence when he entered the
service of King Lamoni. Ammon chose to be the king's
servant and upon the first test of loyalty, when "a certain
number of the Lamanites" (Alma 17:27) scattered the
flocks, Ammon saw his opportunity and took it.

He positioned himself so he could exert influence. In
this case, he had an opportunity to prove his loyalty to
the king. Given that goal, Ammon was thrilled when the
"certain number" did their mischief. The scriptures
record the scattering of the flocks:

"Now when Ammon saw this his heart was swollen

within him with joy; for, said he, I will show forth my power unto these my fellow-servants, or the power which is in me, in restoring these flocks unto the king, that I may win the hearts of these my fellow-servants, that I may lead them to believe in my words.

"And it came to pass that he flattered them by his words, saying: My brethren, be of good cheer and let us go in search of the flocks, and we will gather them together and bring them back unto the place of water; and thus we will preserve the flocks unto the king and he will not slay us" (Alma 17:29, 31).

Ammon then led out, "and they did follow Ammon, and they rushed forth with much swiftness and did head the flocks of the king, and did gather them together again to the place of water" (Alma 17:32). It was upon their second attempt at theft that Ammon had to "contend with these men who do scatter our flocks" (Alma 17:33). He "smote off as many of their arms as were lifted against him, and they were not a few" (Alma 17:38).

It is certainly true that Ammon's actions got the attention of his fellow servants. I submit, however, that if Ammon had not desired to exert influence, he might have handled the entire situation differently. Influence, as Ammon's story shows, may not be obvious to those who watch actions only. Still, it often is a powerful part of getting results.

When King Lamoni heard his servants' report, "he was astonished exceedingly" (Alma 18:2). His astonishment was two-fold: 1) the testimony of his servants "to the things which they had seen" and 2) "the faithfulness of Ammon in preserving his flocks" (Alma 18:2).

For their part, the servants reported, ". . . Whether he [Ammon] be the Great Spirit or a man, we know not; but this much we do know, that he cannot be slain by the enemies of the king; neither can they scatter the king's flocks when he is with us, because of his expertness and great strength; therefore, we know that he is a friend to the king" (Alma 18:3). They testified of a role that allowed Ammon enormous influence when it came time to talk with the king.

It would undoubtedly have been most memorable to watch Ammon in action, but I believe that he was never better than when he exerted righteous influence. Ammon's expertness was much more than his ability to wield a sword. He had the gift of influence, that unique ability to make his presence and message felt.

When Ammon completed his tasks as a servant by caring for the king's horses and chariots, Lamoni was "more astonished, because of the faithfulness of Ammon, saying: Surely there has not been any servant among all my servants that has been so faithful as this man; for even he doth remember all my commandments to execute them" (Alma 18:10). At that point, Ammon had the king's full attention, and what was even more important, the king was then ready to hear Ammon's message.

Influence is like that—a steady, pervasive power of its own. When I think of the sentence, "He/She has been a good influence on me," I generally think of people who have shown the way, often without being much aware of it. Sometimes, like Ammon, these people of influence position themselves to make their message felt.

Joseph Smith taught, "No power or influence can or

ought to be maintained by virtue of the priesthood, only by persuasion, by long-suffering, by gentleness and meekness, and by love unfeigned;" (D&C 121:41). Influence can indeed be maintained by power, but it is at its most powerful when it is exercised with a loving motive.

The influential do not necessarily hold the most important positions although they may do the most important work. They may not be the most articulate, although they may have the most important things to say. The influential are those who care enough to follow through, those whose daily lives preach their sermons, those who preach and teach truth.

In my judgment, influence is such a mighty tool that even negative influences can affect our behavior. When I was just out of college, I lived in Boston. There I encountered the world of mass transit and found that the daily commute could dull the senses in more ways than one. I recall one icy winter day-trip. Laden with dripping woolens and shopping bags, I embarked on a forty-five-minute bus ride home. As it happened, a woman from my ward was on the same bus. I was delighted to see a friendly face and to have some conversation during that interminable ride. Fortunately, the bench on which she was seated cleared soon after I boarded, and I sat down beside her, dumping my parcels around my tired feet.

When an older woman got on the bus, I scrunched up my aching toes, rose and offered her my seat, a behavior I'd been taught at home by my mother. The woman mumbled her thanks and tumbled into the seat. She got off several stops later, and I sank back onto the bench. My friend turned to me and said, "You'll do that your first few months here. But you'll soon get over it."

I was rather stunned. In her own way, my friend exerted a big influence on me, for she made me aware of a truth about some choices I might otherwise have ignored. That experience has proven to be a valuable object lesson.

Influence, that often unseen persuader, remains one of the most powerful tools in our arsenals if we use it well. As Belle Spafford said and Ammon demonstrated, influence properly exercised opens doors in ways nothing else can.

J IS FOR JUDGMENT

J is also for Joan, because following in the footsteps of Joan of Arc and showing good judgment have much in common. My philosophy is that we should always use good judgment, especially to act prudently on our impulses to save the world.

Joan of Arc did a marvelous thing in rallying her countrymen to save France. She stood by her beliefs at the expense of her life. Her integrity, her tenacity, her leadership, her valor are laudable.

In these times live equally laudable souls who periodically emulate Joan of Arc in their families, callings, jobs, and friendships. These good souls, whom I call Joans of Arc, Junior, strive to rescue others, to right the wrongs, to command the issues, to root out the evils, to overcome the problems, in short, to fix things. These folks, of whom I am one, tend to don battle armor, pick up banners, and rush up the nearest hill as if we, like Joan of Arc, could make it all right.

While there is much good to be said for those willing to lead the fight, I suggest that those of us who quickly become a Joan of Arc, Junior would be well advised to proceed with careful thought, for being Joan of Arc, Junior, is serious business that always requires sound judgment. Each and every Joan of Arc, Junior must choose battles carefully. For where there is a battle, there is usually a war, and where there is a war, there are hills on which blood will be shed. Much wisdom is demonstrated by keeping one's banner furled and one's best judgment in evidence until the battlefield has been thoroughly studied.

Through many experiences, like the following, I have learned to survey the situation. A bit ago, I served on a Young Women camp planning committee. We were new to our callings, eager to serve, anxious to please. As our planning began, it wasn't long before each ward comment got treated as if it were an urgent plea. When a fledgling camp director said, "I don't think we'll have enough to do on Thursday night," the committee as a whole took to planning and creating and correcting with zeal. "Got a thought? The stake will finish it for you." seemed to be our motto.

It wasn't long before we ran amuck. Some ward leaders wanted more stake activities, some wanted fewer. Some wanted to begin camp on Tuesday, some wanted to start on Wednesday. Their disparate opinions and requests went on and on. By acting as if we could and should fix every problem, resolve every issue, and direct every leader, we had created a monster of voracious expectations. That monster breathed fire on us, as we stood on the crest of the hill to camp with our flags waving. We had rushed into the fray, but we had not surveyed the field. In our rush to forward momentum, we had ignored such crucial factors as the necessity to evaluate needs and resources; worse, we had completely overlooked the need to respectfully counsel with the stake and ward leaders. We found ourselves in an escalating battle of wills—all the consequence of our poor judgment.

Before the differing perspectives about camp became

a war of wills, the planning committee came to a screeching halt. We took off our "stake to the rescue" armor and reassessed. It was painfully evident that by telling each ward we'd "fix" their problems, we'd given conflicting signals, for the wards did not all want the same things. We had weakened ward leadership by insisting they should rely on us for every solution. We had also alienated a few leaders who did not appreciate what they considered to be officious meddling by our committee. Our conclusion? Poor judgment equals poor results.

During our own self-reckoning, we thought about Jeremiah's plea, "Oh Lord, correct me, but with judgment . . ." (Jeremiah 10:24). It didn't take long for us to see that our Joan of Arc, Junior urges had gotten out of control. We were not helping the ward leaders, we were doing their jobs. We agreed that the ward leaders needed to lead the charge. We needed to act as resources and quite grabbing the banners out of the ward leaders' hands. We regrouped and handled events in better ways thereafter.

Knowing when to pick up the colors if they sag and when to hand the drooping flag to someone else is an art. That kind of judgment requires prayer, thought, and planning. It also demands a good understanding of the truth that sometimes we lead, sometimes we follow. Even if we own all the armor and know how to wave the banner with distinction, we should not always rush to the forefront.

Nephi wrote of his own life experience, "And it came to pass that as I, Nephi, went forth to slay food, behold, I did break my bow . . . and after I did break my bow, behold, my brethren were angry with me because of the

loss of my bow, for we did obtain no food" (1 Nephi
16:18). Hunting was abysmal, the familial pressures
intense. Things "began to be exceedingly difficult" (1
Nephi 16:21). In fact, Nephi uses the words "suffering,"
"affliction," "sorrowful" to describe this experience. The
situation was so bad that even Lehi "began to murmur
against the Lord his God" (1 Nephi 16:20).

It seems to me that in this difficult situation, Nephi
showed excellent judgment by respecting roles. He, the
hunter, made a new weapon. He asked his father, the
patriarch, for counsel about where to hunt.

When Nephi armed himself with his new bow, he
"said unto [his] father: Whither shall I go to obtain
food?" (1 Nephi 16:23). Lehi inquired of the Lord and
was "truly chastened because of his murmuring against
the Lord, insomuch that he was brought down into the
depths of sorrow" (1 Nephi 16:25).

Nephi made the point that "by small means the Lord
can bring about great things" (1 Nephi 16:29) before he
went to the mountain to slay much-needed food. Lehi
was the patriarch and leader; Nephi was the son and
hunter. When each fulfilled his role, no matter how
small, great things came to pass.

That is the way of Joan of Arc, Junior, types of
behavior. In their place, they inspire the souls of men
and women. Out of place, they make people out of sorts.

Our zealous urges to fix everything must be carefully
considered and wisely implemented, else we do injury to
the agency and assignments of others. We are well-
advised to keep our banners repaired but unfurled and
our armor ready but closeted until the battle and the
judgments are right.

K IS FOR KINDNESS

When I watch people behave in kind ways, it warms my heart because I know the practitioners are sincere in their desire to be charitable, to be meek, to be Christ-like.

Kind, charitable, meek people are spiritually "drug free," which means they always remember that their words and actions affect others. I know people who have anesthetized themselves. They will not see that their behavior affects other people in very personal ways. Such people may be nice enough, but they are not charitable.

Like Amulek, each of us may have occasion to say, "Nevertheless, I did harden my heart, for I was called many times and I would not hear; therefore I knew concerning these things, yet I would not know . . ." (Alma 10:6). The Lord would have us "know" that although being pleasant is nice, being kind, charitable, and meek remains essential.

A willful "I would not know" reminds us of Jonah. He seems to have picked up an interesting stick when he chose to flee Tarshish because he didn't like his calling. That end of the stick was willful disobedience. Whether he knew it or not, the other end was his discontent that he didn't get his own way. Jonah became "very angry" that the Lord chose to "spare Ninevah" (Jonah 4:1,11). He seemed focused on a lost gourd while he ignored lost souls. In his hands, that stick, no matter how he held it, was a weapon of disobedience and discontent, not a tool of kindness and meekness.

Kind people are meek. It seems to me that, in fact, meekness underlies most kind behavior. Kind souls have a clarity of internal vision that they choose to cultivate. No fogs or stupors pervade their consciousness for long.

The four standard works all contain this clause: "The meek shall inherit the earth." I consider these six words to be among the most hopeful doctrines of the kingdom. Imagine a world full of men and women who are loving and kind because they choose to do what is right. That is indeed a celestial kingdom.

Meekness represents a desire to become pure, that is, to become like Christ. The Savior said, "Take my yoke upon you, and learn of me; for I am meek and lowly in heart: and ye shall find rest unto your souls" (Matt. 11:29). The yoke is worth taking on, for our meek Savior rewards the obedient shouldering of our burdens with peace that pervades the soul. If the Savior is meek, if peace follows the meek, then let us choose the triumvirate of meekness, charity, and kindness.

Being kind, becoming charitable and meek—these are very private rigors. Like being baptized, praying, and becoming a woman or man of covenant, embodying kindness is something each of us does individually, within the chambers of our own souls.

Sometimes I ponder how my own actions and thoughts might be more like Jonah's than I care to admit. Periodically, I consider if I've picked up the right stick and how I've used it. For example, I find myself getting irritated quite regularly by how difficult it is to merge onto the freeway. "Why don't they let me in?" I say out loud with some disdain for all those cars and their drivers.

When I am at my most rational and calm, I wonder at my own impatience over such a little thing. But in the throes of the daily commute, I can view the other vehicles as the "enemy." My moderate outrage can become one end of a stick. The other end of it, I find, is my own unwillingness, at such moments, to let cars in front of me.

To use the Savior's metaphor, I also find that the yoke He asks me to bear sits much more comfortably when I determine to apply myself kindly to the tasks at hand. If I think of my commute time as an occasion to listen to the scripture or catch up on the news or gather my thoughts for the day or pray with thanksgiving for guidance, I can kindly let others in and out of the lanes I temporarily inhabit.

Kindness has a million faces. It is so antithetical to this world and so critical to our commute through it. It shows itself as we speak politely to strangers on the phone, as we sooth a child's anxiety, as we assist an aging parent, as we deal with disagreements in the workplace. Far too untapped and unappreciated, kindness represents our commitment to Christ and remains one happy evidence of our desires to become charitable and meek.

L IS FOR LAUGHTER

When everyone was still at home, we'd gather around a Queen Anne chair in my parents' living room for family prayer. Often it was late in the evening before everyone convened. My memory is that in most cases the prayer didn't actually begin until everyone had a chance to tell a few stories about the day's events.

There we'd be, circling the "prayer chair," as we called it, on our knees. Generally, there was some hearty laughter over someone's tale. The laughter would end, and the prayer would begin. I think the good cheer of those family moments shared around the prayer chair enhanced our conversations with the Lord.

"Everyone needs a laughing place," Brer Rabbit said in the Uncle Remus stories. And he was so right. Laughter can be both relief and refreshment, and everyone needs a spot in which positive, wholesome laughter is fostered and welcomed.

The famous scripture in Ecclesiastes says, "To every thing there is a season, and a time to every purpose under the heaven: "A time to weep, and a time to laugh..." (Ecclesiastes. 3:1, 4).

This is so true. Laughter does indeed have its time and place.

I used to have a quasi-space map of the continental United States on the back door of my office. Every time I closed my door, there it was, a completely black piece of paper with a white outline of the contiguous states. White dots, sometimes blotches in large metropolitan areas, represented the lights of cities and towns. I'd look at the few pinpoints of light where I lived and chuckle as I reminded myself that my world was not the world.

Good humor is cleansing, isn't it? If we don't have buddies with whom we can enjoy a robust laugh, we might be well advised to expand our pool of friends. I crave the perspective borne of good humor, and I am grateful for the friends who bring me insights and laughter, which often go together.

"Isn't that funny?" is a favorite family line. Our mutual liking for a good laugh binds us together. Invariably laughter serves as the condiment for whatever we serve at every family get together. These points of humor add to our relationships and often prove to be gifts that keep on giving. Funny family lines bind us and remind us of the times and seasons of our lives. When Grandma quotes a grandson's two year-old humor, and he is now fourteen, he knows his grandmother has been listening to him for well over a decade.

I maintain that laughing places can be both external and internal. An external laughing place, like our family prayer chair, can be a friend's home, a regular telephone call, or a favorite café. Wherever wholesome laughter awaits, that's a fine laughing place. A sense of humor is, of course, the internal laughing place. In times of crisis or sadness, that sense of humor heals and salves.

This recent family experience reminded me of how helpful my laughing place can be.

Mom was away on an extended trip when I got a phone call from my Aunt Verginia. "Aunt Mad is bad, and your mother has all the legal papers. Can you meet me at the care center?" Aunt Mad is short for Aunt Madeline, my grandmother's youngest sister and my great aunt, age ninety-five. Sometimes she thinks she has a glass eye that she keeps in a cup of water by her bed. Actually, she still has her own eyes; it's her teeth she keeps in the water. She was one of the cheeriest souls I've ever known, but dementia has taken its toll.

When I arrived at the care center, I could instantly see that Aunt Mad was bad. The rattle in her chest sounded like pneumonia to me. The nurse confirmed it, so Aunt Verginia and I determined that a vigil of sorts was in order. Days went on, and Aunt Mad slid in and out of reality, often not knowing who she was.

On one Saturday when she was particularly bad, I came to visit. Ruby, in the next bed, had also slid downhill during Aunt Mad's illness. "Hello, Ruby," I said as I sat by Aunt Mad's bed and took her hand. Ruby called to me, "Be sure to clean those chickens good." Then she launched into a long dialogue with her children, long since grandparents themselves, but little ones in Ruby's mind at that moment.

Aunt Mad stirred. "A man came to see me," she said. "He was all in white."

Immediately I thought it might be a courier from the other side, and I devoutly wished she had taken his hand, no matter who he was, and let him help her get Home. "Was it your dad, Aunt Mad?"

"I don't know."

"One of your brothers?"

"He was so handsome, but I don't know who he was."

I hoped and prayed that it had been a messenger from beyond the veil and that he would soon return. These somber, tender thoughts congregated in my mind, bringing tears to my eyes. Just then the door of the room opened with a flourish. In strode a young woman bedecked in a bridal gown and veil. Followed by her mother and a nurse, the young woman went to Aunt Mad's bed and gave her a big kiss.

"Are you an angel?" Aunt Mad asked.

The nurse spoke for the bride. "It's Teresa," she responded. "Don't you remember? She's getting married today, and you're invited to the wedding." It came to me that Mom had said two of the care center workers were marrying each other. I looked out the door and sure enough, wheelchair after wheelchair was heading down the hall to the atrium where, I assumed, the ceremony would take place. Pushing one of the chairs was Jose, a very nice-looking man, today dressed all in white. He was one of Aunt Mad's favorites at the center, and he waved a greeting to the wedding party as he passed.

"Isn't she a beautiful bride?" The nurse propped Aunt Mad up to get a better look. "Don't you want to go to the wedding?" She began to pull the blankets aside.

"Congratulations," I said to the girl in white, "You are a beautiful bride. And I am sure Ruby and Madeline think so too." I moved to Aunt Mad's bed. "Look at Aunt Mad," I whispered to the very distracted nurse who was clearly in the throes of wedding mania. "She is definitely not wedding material today."

"Oh well. Oh yes." the nurse spluttered as the mother of the bride straightened the veil that was draped all over Aunt Mad, who by then was listing dangerously near the edge of the bed. The bridal party happily whooshed out the door, and I quickly readjusted Aunt Mad in her bed. She was almost instantly asleep.

I mumbled to myself, "I know who that messenger was, and he was definitely not from the other side." I waved at Jose as he called to Aunt Mad as he made his way down the hall to bring another guest to the wedding.

Yes, everyone needs a laughing place, for there are times when only a laugh will do.

M IS FOR MIDST

There are times in life when we know we dropped an anchor, yet we feel adrift. We ponder the scriptures, yet we wonder at life's injustices. We relish the calm of the temple, yet we grow so quickly restive when we return to daily life. We pray with zeal, yet we weary as the answers seem to come slowly and hard. We seek calm, yet life whirls like a maelstrom.

Like the Jaredites, we have seasons at sea. Reassuring landmarks sometimes set with the sun, and the boats in which we sail on moonless nights may have been "many times buried in the depths of the sea, because of the mountain waves which broke upon them, and also the great and terrible tempest which were caused by the fierceness of the wind" (Ether 6:6). It is during those voyages, while the waves roar and buffet us, that the questions loom large. We're engrossed in battening down the hatches, wondering all the while if the whole ship is sinking.

Many of us are in the middle:

> Middle age.
> Middle weight
> Middle of the road.
> Middle generation.
> Middle income.

Day in, day out we find ourselves mid-life, mid-sentence, mid-marriage, mid-parenting, mid-career, mid-thought, even mid-muddle. Even as we stand mid-ships, our boats sometimes tip alarmingly.

In the midst, mortality is confusing, difficult, and oh, so tiring.

But it is more.

After our Savior fed the five thousand, ". . . straightway Jesus constrained his disciples to get into a ship, and to go before him unto the other side, while he sent the multitudes away.

"And when he had sent the multitudes away, he went up into a mountain apart to pray: and when the evening was come, he was there alone.

"But the ship was now in the midst of the sea, tossed with waves: for the wind was contrary.

"And in the fourth watch of the night Jesus went unto them, walking on the sea.

"And when the disciples saw him walking on the sea, they were troubled, saying, It is a spirit; and they cried out for fear.

"But straightway Jesus spake unto them, saying, Be of good cheer; it is I; be not afraid."

Like the disciples of Christ, our ships are in the midst of the sea. Cork-like, our vessels may bob out of our control. But to us, as to His disciples of old, the Savior speaks. "Be of good cheer; it is I; be not afraid" (Matt. 14:22-27).

Joseph Smith wrote from the Liberty Jail:

> You know, brethren, that a very large ship is bene-fitted very much by a very small help in the time of a

storm, by being kept workways with the wind and the waves.

Therefore, dearly beloved brethren, let us cheerfully do all things that lie in our power; and then may we stand still, with the utmost assurance, to see the salvation of God, and for his arm to be revealed (D&C 123:16-17).

His message in those turbulent times echoes the Savior. Truly, it is the Master who is our real anchor no matter how the waves threaten to swamp our boats. Even when the rough seas of life swamp us, we can take cheer and courage. With surety, with safety, in fact with utter assurance, we can focus not at our damp decks, but on the Lord.

For in the midst of it all, our Savior reigns.

N IS FOR NAME

What does your name mean to you? Does it connect you with a relative whose name you bear? Does your surname have a unique meaning? Does it have significance because of your ancestry or land of birth?

Names are important. When King Benjamin gathered his people together to hear his last message, he said: "I shall give this people a name that thereby they may be distinguished above all the people which the Lord God hath brought out of the land of Jerusalem . . . and I give unto them a name that never shall be blotted out, except it be through transgression" (Mosiah 1:11-12).

King Benjamin told his people that the name they would bear was the name of our Savior. The king explained:

> Because of the covenant which ye have made ye shall be called the children of Christ, his sons, and his daughters; for behold, this day he hath spiritually begotten you; for ye say that your hearts are changed through faith on his name; therefore, ye are born of him and have become his sons and his daughters. . . . There is no other name given whereby salvation cometh; therefore, I would that ye should take upon you the name of Christ, . . . This is the name that I said I should give unto you that never should be blotted out, except it be through transgression . . . I would

that ye should remember to retain the name written always in your hearts . . . that ye hear and know the voice by which ye shall be called and also the name by which he shall call you" (Mosiah 5:7-8, 11-12).

It seems significant to me that at the end of his speech, King Benjamin had the names taken of all those who had entered into the covenant with God to keep His commandments. (See Mosiah 6:1.)

Each time we take the sacrament and renew our covenants, we take the name of the Savior upon us again. The blessing on the bread, as recorded in Moroni 4:3, states, "We ask thee in the name of thy son, Jesus Christ, to bless and sanctify this bread . . . that they are willing to take upon them the name of thy son."

The Savior gave the Nephite apostles authority to "call on the Father in my name in mighty prayer . . . ye shall give the Holy Ghost and in my name shall ye give it . . ." (Moroni 2:2).

With good reason, parents drill into their children the importance of acting honorably upon the names they bear. To bear a family name means something. I understood this concept better when I helped a family member take care of some legal matters and needed a power of attorney. This right to legally act in someone else's name was not that easy to obtain. I discovered a very long list of what I could and could not do with that power. I was struck by the responsibility I had undertaken in acting in another's name.

If it is a major commitment to take on another's name legally, if we honor our forebears by giving their names to our children, consider what it means to take upon us the name of our Savior. Doing so is both a sacred and blessed responsibility. And it comforts my soul to know we will never be orphaned spiritually when we will take upon us the name of our Savior.

Our names are not only how we are known. They are more; they soon come to represent what we stand for.

What's in a name? Everything if the name we take upon us is that of our Savior. As we are known by His name, as we take His name upon us, the names by which we are known can bespeak honor, consecration and family strength.

O IS FOR OPEN

Then opened he their understanding, that they might understand the scriptures (Luke 24:45).

Not long ago a woman I know shared a family story about openness. Her younger brother, recently separated from his wife, had returned to the town of their childhood where she and her family were long established. Having no job, he had requested that she allow him to live with her until he could get on his feet.

The two siblings had never been close; in fact, she didn't even like her brother. He'd drifted professionally, personally, and morally, so when she agreed to a two-month stay, it was with great reluctance. It was only a few days before he proved to be a grave trial to her, and all her youthful feelings about him returned full-blown.

In no regard did they see eye to eye or hear ear to ear. After an exceedingly long month of concerted effort, she concluded that he had been switched at birth. He had to be from another planet when he behaved in ways so uncharacteristic of the rest of their family. His words and behavior turned her own family inside out and the household upside down.

She did everything imaginable to create consensus among the small family group—meetings, Family Home Evenings, notes, prayers, food, one-on-one discussions, field trips, etc., etc. Nothing worked.

As always happens in an environment of unresolved contention, things got worse. Determined to endure to the end of her two months' commitment and desperate to improve the collective family disposition, she started reading scriptures when everyone sat together for dinner, hoping the words and meanings would have a soothing influence on everyone. On more than one occasion she read, "And Jesus . . . said unto them, Every kingdom divided against itself is brought to desolation; and every city or house divided against itself shall not stand:" (Matt. 12:25). Her brother would not hear, he would not cooperate.

The sister persisted in trying to find at least some measure of communication, but her brother grew increasingly sullen and obstinate. No pleading, cajoling, lecturing, humoring, chatting, or directing improved the situation. In fact, the only work he did at home seemed to be designed to undermine her roles as wife, mother, and sister.

Finally, in a moment of desperation, she stopped trying. For several days she said nothing but spent time prayerfully pondering the circumstance. It came to her that while she was adept at reading the scriptures to others, she was not demonstrating much openness to understanding the message of the scriptures or the needs of her brother. Over and over in her mind, she had rehearsed her brother's faults. Never had she been open to a broader understanding of his circumstances or his feelings.

She reread the scripture:

> Ye have heard that it hath been said, Thou shalt love thy neighbor, and hate thine enemy.
> But I say unto you, Love your enemies, bless them

that curse you, do good to them that hate you, and pray for them which despitefully use you, and persecute you (Matt. 5:43-44).

That scripture spelled out the principle clearly. What she needed was an understanding of how to implement it. She reread Paul:

When I was a child, I spake as a child, I understood as a child, I thought as a child: but when I became a man, I put away childish things.

For now we see through a glass, darkly; but then face to face: now I know in part; but then shall I know even as also I am known (1 Corinthians 13:11-12).

She was determined to put away her childish feelings and become open to understanding her brother as he was now. If he left the next week, the end of the agreed upon two months, she wanted him to leave knowing he was loved.

After a particularly testy encounter several days later, she took a different course of action than she had ever tried before. She ran to the store and bought her brother a tie, which she had beautifully gift wrapped. With negative feelings still running high but a great desire to be open in her heart, she knocked on his bedroom door. Wincing at his sullen response, she reluctantly shuffled into his room. He glowered at her as she sat down in his chair and handed him the gift.

Clearly expecting another confrontation, he looked positively bemused. His surprise and the moment of silence that ensued gave her a chance to speak from her heart. With a catch in her throat, she said, "I want you to know that although we do not agree, I wish you well. There is no malice in my heart towards you. I love you, Sam, and I want you to be happy. I am so sorry we do not understand each other better."

He remained speechless for several minutes, then responded, "Thank you."

That incident did not fix the situation, nor did she expect it to. It did succeed in doing something wonderful though. Once she had communicated with him out of love, she was more open to him. She began to look with more appreciation at his skills and with more compassion on his weaknesses. He became more gentle in his responses to her and her husband and children. The entire family calmed down.

While still far from perfect, the family situation was better. My friend and her husband invited her brother to stay with them another month.

As she tells the tale, the best learning for her came when she decided to be open to understanding. Scriptures she'd read for years took on life for her when she applied them to a difficult situation in her own life. New insights flowed and old feelings dissipated.

She found out how necessary it is to be open to understanding. She found not only that she did not know it all, but also that she did not know her brother. Her openness encouraged his, and together they gained understanding they had never shared before. This mutual understanding fostered the type of relationship they'd never had—a relationship based upon being open.

P is for Prayer

I was leading a group of twenty high school students on a three-week trip through the former Soviet Union. "Perestroika" was not yet a reality, and the republics were not independent. Our last leg began with a train ride from Kiev to Budapest. It would last twenty-two hours and involve a stop at the border checkpoint about 2 A.M. I warned the students not to be alarmed when the train stopped and to expect guards to look in their compartments, maybe even through their luggage.

The trip went flawlessly into the night, and right on schedule the train halted. I heard the guards coming several cars away. Their manner of slamming open sleeping compartment doors gave ample notice they meant business. When they entered our car slinging their machines guns to their shoulders, several of them slapped all the lights on and gestured impatiently for all the students to stand at attention.

The lead Hungarian soldier, probably no more than twenty-two years-old himself, demanded our passports and visas in practiced but unclear English. His perusal of our documents ended with a blunt request for our visas. "You have them," I gestured to the handful of papers.

"Your visas now," his voice threatened. The senior Soviet guard and several of his men, hearing the tone in the Hungarian's voice, came over. Obviously uncomfortable with each other, the Hungarians and Russians huddled around me as I tried to explain that they had all of our documents. The Soviet soldier, no older than the Hungarian, asked none too gently for our visas also. When I again said I had no more papers to give them, they drew into a tighter circle around me, and their talk grew more animated.

We were in trouble. I didn't have to understand Hungarian or Russian to know that. Fortunately, Susan, another teacher accompanying me, possessed a steady hand and wise head. "We can't get off this train without a fight," she whispered to me. "Once they kick us off, we'll be stuck. We don't know where we are, and we have no means of communicating with the West. We'll have to pitch a very large fit so that whoever oversees these guards knows we're here." I instinctively knew she was right.

Two hours later, well aware that we were there, several furious senior guards herded us onto a cracked, crumbling cement platform while the rest of the troops hurled our suitcases out the train windows into the surrounding pasture. Whatever animosity the troops had for each other was forgotten in their anger toward us.

In a final huff, the train pulled out and we huddled in the cool breeze under the lone forty-watt light bulb swinging slowly on its long cord. The breeze told us cows were close, even if people weren't. Other than the scant lights emanating from the small train station behind us, we could see no signs of life. Fog rose from the dank grass.

We moved into the station and sent the students looking for a place to sleep. The resourceful students found an empty customs room. We took it over. The one attendant on duty seemed not to care what anyone did as long as he didn't have to leave his chair behind the bar. Susan and I quickly surmised that we were incommunicado, just as she'd predicted. No fax. A telegraph the attendant wouldn't let us use. Only one phone locked in the tiny Intourist office, was a local link to what was then the national and sole travel agency of the Soviet Union.

In the dark customs room I urged the students and other teachers to cover the filthy floor or benches with their towels and jackets and to get some sleep. It was just after 4:00 A.M. and the Intourist office, our one link to the outside, wouldn't open for hours.

Already subdued, the group quickly quieted. Alone, I began pacing the floor. Each step seemed to bring a greater realization of our frightening circumstance. I looked at those twenty faces as I walked by them. Lying on towels, propped on suitcases, they had done well in a difficult moment. I felt proud and protective of them. My responsibility for them weighed as heavy as the dirty air of the room. I was scared to death.

In that midnight silence, I prayed earnestly. I knew the Lord was aware of us. He knew we needed help, and I asked Him for it. I begged Him to help us rally our faith, although we were members of many churches. I prayed that He would pour out His spirit upon those we would speak with in the morning and soften their hearts towards us. I beseeched Him to bless Susan and me to speak for our small group in the right way. Over and over I prayed. Through the night and past the dawn, I prayed.

A story came to mind. I thought about Parley P. Pratt
in Richmond Jail at the same time Joseph Smith was in
Liberty Jail. The story is rather involved, but the end of
it was what moved me. Parley and his fellows followed
spiritual promptings and executed their escape from jail.
I remembered in my own words what I quote here in
Parley's words:

> In this, as in most other fields of battle, where
> liberty and life depend on the issue, every one under-
> stood the part assigned to him and exactly filled it.
> Mr. Follett was to give the door a sudden pull, and
> fling it wide open the moment the key was turned. Mr.
> Phelps being well skilled in wrestling was to press out
> foremost, and come in contact with the jailer; I was to
> follow in the centre, and Mr. Follett, who held the
> door, was to bring up the rear, while sister Phelps was
> to pray.
>
> No sooner was the key turned than the door was
> seized by Mr. Follett with both hands; and with his
> foot placed against the wall, he soon opened a
> passage, which was in the same instant filled by Mr.
> Phelps, and followed by myself and Mr. Follett. The
> old jailer strode across the way, and stretched out his
> arms like Bunyan's Apollion, or like the giant Despair
> in Doubting Castle, but all to no purpose. One or two
> leaps brought us to the bottom of the stairs, carrying
> the old gentleman with us headlong, helter skelter,
> while . . . Mrs. Phelps exclaimed, "O Lord God of
> Israel, thou canst help" (Parley P. Pratt, The
> Autobiography of Parley P. Pratt, Chapter. 32, quoted
> in *A Believing People*, edited by Richard H. Cracroft
> and Neal E. Lambert, Brigham Young University
> Press, 1974, pp. 58-59).

What stuck in my mind was the line, "O Lord God of Israel, thou canst help." I determined that all of us must pull together spiritually if we were to successfully escape this place. It mattered not what church, if any, my fellow travelers belonged to. It mattered not if they had any experience with prayer. We must rally our joined spiritual strength, such as it was. They must pray while Susan and I executed our escape.

As the rustle of travelers sounded through the walls, I opened the door. Morning had broken, clear and bright. Happily, I spotted a tray of fresh bread and some mineral water—breakfast! Soon, with bread and water in hand, we gratefully faced the day. Before we ate, I gathered the company together. I thanked them for their cooperation and maturity, and then explained, "Susan and I must meet with the Intourist agent in a few minutes. That person is our ticket home. We need your help even though you won't be in the room with us. I am asking all of you to join in a prayer now because we need the Lord's blessings. We're going to thank Him for this food and for our safety, and we're going to ask for His help so we can get out of here quickly.

"While Susan and I are meeting with the agent, I want you to pray. That's your job, just as mine is to talk to the Intourist agent." I charged the remaining adult to be sure they had another prayer while Susan and I met with the agent. We bowed our heads, and I prayed with the zeal of my soul. Then Susan and I headed off.

Our colossal resistance on the train paid off. The woman sitting behind the Intourist desk had been informed of our situation. She spoke no English, but she did speak some French. Susan spoke no French but knew some Russian. I had never gotten my tongue around French very well, but I could understand it. We communicated with each other and in gentle tones, with a few words written for clarification, we worked out a plan.

Our tri-lingual conversation included an apology from a senior Russian guard, who stood before us, hat in hand, speaking respectfully. I didn't have to understand a word to know he was sorry we'd been waylaid and that the young men on the night shift might be spending their next evening cleaning up some of the origin of the bucolic aroma of the place.

In a short version of an involved story, the Russians bussed us to the border, the Hungarians sold us new visas and train tickets, for the young guards had taken our other ones. After hours of waiting and memorable adventures foraging for food, we boarded a train for Budapest. I hadn't slept in thirty-six hours, but I didn't begin to relax until everyone was settled, most of them napping as the train hurtled west.

Breathing deep of the fresh air, I stood by the open train window, watching beautiful Hungary rush by. I have never been any more grateful for prayer than I was at that moment. Nor had the restored gospel ever been more dear to me than it was as our weary group disembarked in Budapest.

That daring escapade in rural Ukraine and Hungary bore witness to me that we can take the Lord at his word. The Lord will lead us by the hand and give us answer to our prayers (D&C 112:10). He hears and answers prayers, he can and does help.

Q IS FOR QUIETNESS

"And the work of righteousness shall be peace; and the effect of righteousness quietness and assurance for ever" (Isaiah. 32:17). Quietness and assurance. The words themselves soothe.

To be alive today is to know what it means to say, "Master, the tempest is raging." The Savior's response, "Peace, be still," suggests much more than a temporary reprieve from trials or boredom. His command also means that the quietness and assurance he promised us can remain through mortality's many stormy and windless days.

Our Savior explained:

> I came forth from the Father, and am come into the world: again, I leave the world, and go to the Father.
>
> Behold, the hour cometh, yea, is now come, that ye [His disciples] shall be scattered, every man to his own, and shall leave me alone: and yet I am not alone, because the Father is with me.
>
> These things I have spoken unto you, that in me ye might have peace. In the world ye shall have tribulation: but be of good cheer; I have overcome the world" (John 16:28, 32-33).

Because the gospel has been restored, my questions, my quest can result in quietness—and assurance.

Several years ago I attended a Relief Society retreat. As an opening activity, the leader asked each dinner group to hold a "Q and A" session. She didn't mean questions and answers though. She meant *quietness* and *assurance*. Each of us was asked to share something that brought quietness and assurance to her life. Prayer, scripture study, temple attendance, service, meditation, nature walks, or talks with friends.

Isaiah's scripture says that the effect of righteous living is quietness and assurance. Like you, I know those whose lives are so refined that their very presence is soothing. A ward Young Women president I know is possessed of such a peaceful spirit that those around her often respond accordingly. Her quiet ways and words seem to assure leaders and youth that they are loved and valued.

In a choppy, blustering world, quietness and assurance are unique by any standard. They are a sharp contrast to the bombast of media, for example. When we encounter so many environments in which louder is better, it is nice to know that quietness and assurance can be our everlasting partners.

I find that quietness and assurance are equally needful in times of deluge and drought. Sometimes the world holds too little, and the resultant boredom and ennui sap our spiritual strength. At such times it is more than nice to know that righteous living bears its fruit, even if the seeds lie dormant for a season.

I am aware of a man whose entire life was filled with service and society. His profession was public relations, and his Church callings revolved around people. As an elders' quorum president, bishop, stake president, etc., he spent his time caring for others. His wife had the same bent, and they entertained often. As a mission president, he connected with people who continued to visit him every time they were in proximity. Father of a large family, he was always engaged in his children's many activities.

A sudden change in fortunes altered much of his life. Due to international business concerns, his employer floundered and forced him to take early retirement. His children left home for missions, marriage, and graduate school. His high council calling ended a mere month before his job did. From a tornado of activity, he was reduced to a few puffs.

What sustained him was the quietness and assurance he reaped from years of righteous living. Many years of good works had grown deep spiritual roots in his life. The spiritual limbs of a giant testimony sheltered him, even enveloped him in quietness and assurance as he plowed yet new fields.

Sometimes the world holds too much. I observed a wonderful mother and father who had so much and so many in their household that they never seemed to land. They were people who radiated quietness and assurance. I marveled at this, knowing their lifestyle.

I asked them once how they found such peace during such a riotous season in their lives. Both responded with the same message. "This time is not really so different from the years when we began our lives together, and our children were young." I was surprised and asked how that could be so when their schedules were so dissimilar from what they had been.

"Our priorities are the same. Our daily routines are much the same. Our communication with family members has always been a high priority. Our Church service is steady. We live as we always have, and we experience the peace we always have." Their response made me think.

What I realized is that their quietness and assurance was not based on having family surround them or being on vacation or finding themselves in social demand. They had learned that in cases of lots or little, they could expect quietness and assurance to be results of daily righteous living.

What an assuring reality that is. How quiet and calm we can feel with such knowledge. Quietness and assurance—gentle, calming doctrine and words.

R IS FOR RIGHTEOUS

Righteous desires should be cherished, even when they long pre-date the blessings we seek. Our desires, when righteous, do so much to settle and steady us. The scriptures teach the significance of our desires, righteous and otherwise.

The Savior said:

> And by their desires and their works you shall know them" (D&C 18:38).

Alma, in his missionary zeal, exclaimed:

> I ought not to harrow up in my desires, the firm decree of a just God, for I know that he granteth unto men according to their desire . . .
>
> Yea, and I know that good and evil have come before all men . . . he that knoweth good and evil, to him it is given according to his desires, whether he desireth good or evil, life or death, joy or remorse of conscience.
>
> Now, seeing that I know these things, why should I desire more than to perform the work to which I have been called? (Alma 29:4-6).

I take these scriptures to mean that our desires classify us. Our righteous desires determine, in large part, where we end up. Given the obvious importance of these righteous desires in propelling us forward in the right direction, it is folly to abdicate them, even if they are long in coming to fruition.

During a time when I served in Relief Society, I was asked to answer a letter my Relief Society president received from a single woman in her thirties. Frustrated about not being married and having her own family, she poured out her heart in this letter. She explained that she'd contributed generously, served faithfully, prayed diligently, attended the temple regularly. The Lord had responded to her with "a great big nothing," she said, as her reward for all her years of faithfulness. She felt she'd given her all, and now she'd given up her righteous desire to be a wife and mother because she hadn't yet married. Worse, she was prepared to abandon her testimony because "the whole church thing seems fruitless."

"Have faith," seemed the proper answer to her plea for counsel. I felt, though, that such a response wouldn't satisfy her. It seemed she wanted to hear something easier—something defined and packaged in all the ways life usually isn't. I thought about Gideon and shared with her his story, as I liken it unto myself.

As we meet Gideon, he is threshing "wheat by the winepress, to hide it from the Midianites."

"And the angel of the Lord appeared unto him, and said unto him, The Lord is with thee, thou mighty man of valour." I take it from Gideon's response that he was none too impressed by that lofty greeting, and he was most unhappy about living as a vassal. His retort:

". . . Oh my Lord, if the Lord be with us, why then is all this befallen us? and where be all his miracles which our fathers told us of, saying, Did not the Lord bring us up from Egypt? but now the Lord hath forsaken us, and delivered us into the hands of the Midianites."

To which the Lord responded, ". . . Go in this thy might, and thou shalt save Israel from the hand of the Midianites: have not I sent thee?"

Gideon replied, ". . . Oh my Lord, wherewith shall I save Israel? behold, my family is poor in Manasseh, and I am the least in my father's house.

"And the Lord said unto him, Surely I will be with thee, and thou shalt smite the Midianites as one man."

Gideon had doubts, so he asked for—and got—a sign. When he finally understood that he had seen an angel, that he had received a calling from the Lord, he feared for his life:

". . . for because I have seen an angel of the Lord face to face.

"And the Lord said unto him, Peace be unto thee; fear not: thou shalt not die."

Gideon's first job was to "throw down the altar of Baal that thy father hath, and cut down the grove that is by it:

"And build an altar unto the Lord" and do sacrifice.

Now I am sure that Gideon felt enormous concern for religious, cultural and personal reasons. Still, to this distant observer it also appears that Gideon took hesitant first steps in his new calling. He was no Superman emerging from the phone booth ready to save the day. "Then Gideon took ten men of his servants, and did as the Lord had said unto him: and so it was, because he feared his father's household, and the men of the city, that he could not do it by day, that he did it by night."

Gideon needed reassurance. Again, he sought a sign,

prefaced by these words, "And Gideon said unto God, If thou wilt save Israel by mine hand, as thou hast said, Behold, I will put a fleece of wool in the floor; and if the dew be on the fleece only, and it be dry upon all the earth beside, then shall I knew that thou wilt save Israel by mine hand, as thou hast said" (Judges 6:11-16, 22-23, 25-27, 36-37). When it was so, Gideon sought yet another sign to verify his calling. Another sign was given.

In the end, after all the hesitation and need for reassurance, with a mere three hundred men Gideon defeated the Midianites, proving that the Lord does deliver His people.

What I love most about Gideon, the hesitant hero, is that he kept on. Like most of us, he sought assurance when he faced unknown challenges that seemed beyond him. He was hesitant, even fearful, about his future. He couldn't choose his circumstances, but he could choose his responses.

Gideon's story tells me that through it all, he retained his righteous desires. He did not give in or give up. He may have paused when he had doubts, but never was he permanently immobilized dissuaded by his fears. He kept after what was his to do, his to be, thereby becoming a tool in our Father's hands, despite all his fits and starts.

That's the level of faith I wanted that good sister to ponder. I wanted her to look deeper, to revalue her righteous desires, to shine them up and let them sparkle in her heart as bright reminders of her beliefs. I sensed that she, like Gideon and all the rest of us, stumbled. But she was still on the path, and she desired what was right. I wanted her to recall the words of our Savior and the

prophets and to reaffirm that her own, heart-felt righteous desires were both gift and opportunity. I longed for
her to consider her righteous desires as wonders to be
cherished and cultivated, and to understand that in
large measure what she did with and about them would
demonstrate her mettle.

And that's what I shared with her—my desire that
she would recognize and hold tight to her own righteous
desires.

S IS FOR SIFT

Several years ago I was trying to find words for a deep feeling I didn't know how to express. Finally, thanks to a General Conference talk given by Elder Neal A. Maxwell, I found my voice. Elder Maxwell quoted Brigham Young:

> "Some do not understand duties which do not coincide with their natural feelings and affections . . . . There are duties which are above affection" (*Journal of Discourses*, 7:65). This rubbing of our natural feelings against the duties above affection creates a cloud of chaff as the wheat of our souls is sifted. The Lord said, "For, lo, I will command, and I will sift the house of Israel among all nations, like as corn is sifted in a sieve, yet shall not the least grain fall upon the earth" (Amos 9:9).

My inexpressible feelings had arisen from personal relationships. I believe that often these most important connections with others prove to be one of life's great sifters, for they force us to grind through issues and immaturities. They show us at our best and worst. They also provide the best experiences in life.

The experiences of Nephi show how relationships can sift us thoroughly. "Behold, it came to pass that I, Nephi, did cry much unto the Lord my God, because of the anger of my brethren.

"But behold, their anger did increase against me, insomuch that they did seek to take away my life.

"Yea, they did murmur against me, saying: Our younger brother thinks to rule over us; and we have had much trial because of him; wherefore, now let us slay him, that we may not be afflicted more because of his words. . . .

"Now I do not write upon these plates all the words which they murmured against me. But it sufficeth me to say, that they did seek to take away my life" (2 Ne. 5:1-4).

Nephi, under directions from the Lord, separated his people from his brethren thereafter, and made this point, "Wherefore, the word of the Lord was fulfilled which he spake unto me, saying that: Inasmuch as they will not hearken unto thy words they shall be cut off from the presence of the Lord. And behold, they were cut off from his presence" (2 Nephi 5:21).

From Brigham Young's thought and Nephi's experiences I learn several things about how sifting occurs in our lives:

1. If we would be faithful followers of the Savior, we must expect conflict between our natural inclinations and our righteous duties. Nephi must have felt extreme emotion at finding himself in a position where he had to separate from his own family members because they sought his life.

2. The Lord does not always answer our prayers in what we might perceive as a straightforward, causal manner. The answers He gives often sift us. Despite Nephi's righteousness, the Lord did

not assuage his brothers' feelings of anger, for example.

3. No matter how events appear to us, the inexorable laws of our Heavenly Father always remain in effect. When Laman and Lemuel and their families disassociated themselves from the Lord, they were cut off from his presence.

From my own experiences, I learn other, equally valuable lessons as I am sifted.

Years ago I worked in a Young Women presidency with two much more seasoned and proficient women than I. Karen, the other counselor, came to the position with years of exceptional Church and professional experience under her belt. This fine woman knew how to get things done with aplomb. Jenny, the president, would rather have been a ward advisor and so stated. Unsettled in the calling, she truly didn't know what to do next. I was a novice, so in the first months I did more observing than anything else.

Karen understood the process of sifting. Her own experiences had taught her the truth of Brigham Young's message about duties and Nephi's trials with errant brothers. She was determined to let the chaff blow away and to save the wheat. What a difference that attitude made to all of us. If she had taken the "I know, and you don't" approach, then we all, like Nephi's older brothers, would have been in peril of being cut off.

Instead, Karen rallied to our help, no matter how she felt about my ineptitude or Jenny's hesitation. My close observation showed that in a thousand small ways this counselor supported her president, respecting her and the position she held. Over and over Jenny and I heard, "What do you need? How can I help? Have you thought about . . . ? We could . . . You did such a great job on . . . I loved what you told the girls at camp about . . ." Praise, support, and love oozed from this woman, all of it most sincere and filled with the Spirit. We all thrived in that environment of love and acceptance.

After several months of observing her, I asked Karen how she had learned those wonderful skills that made her years of experience a blessing rather than a threat to us. "The most important thing," she began, "is that we build the kingdom of God. I've consecrated to do just that. This is my time to be the counselor, not the president, the secretary or the advisor. Besides, the Lord won't bless us if we don't work together, and being at odds is never any fun."

I am sure Karen got frustrated on many occasions, but she chose a duty which may have been beyond affection. Steadily, she stood at Jenny's side as her right hand.

I've talked with both these women in the years since we served together. I've thanked them repeatedly for what they taught me as we were sifted together, like the raw ingredients that when blended and baked make a delicious product. Together, those sisters baked up something very fine.

Sifting is good in more ways than one. It is a process that separates the wheat out and allows proper blending of ingredients. In both senses, sifting makes us better if we are equally willing to part with the chaff of our lives, including our own natural affections on occasion.

T IS FOR TRUTH

I was sitting in an elegant home with the owners, a couple who generously shared it, and in this case with some Young Adult Relief Society leaders. It was late, the training meeting in which we'd all participated was long over. Still, these young sisters lingered.

After a lot of good humor, the conversation turned to the subject most on these women's minds: men and marriage. Young Adult after Young Adult talked about her frustration and fears related to boyfriends and matrimony. Laughter faded, to be replaced by words of longing and hope that spoke much of what stirred in these good women's hearts.

Across from me sat a twenty-four-year-old with angst all over her face. I resonated to that look and felt it to my core when, after a long time of listening, she quietly offered, "I have given up. I feel only despair when I think about marriage." I knew those few words spoke volumes. Tears came to my eyes, and I longed to rush over and give her a hug, to offer words that would calm and assure her.

Just then the host, a man of position in every regard, said, "I guess if you don't have a husband and family, you're living Plan B." I watched that young woman wither. I could not bear the thought of that young woman leaving that home feeling that because she was single, she was relegated to a Plan B life.

Another leader jumped in. "I don't see it that way. If a woman is single, she still has access to great opportunities and blessings. She can receive her endowments, contribute in many places and make a rich, happy life."

Our lovely hostess leaped to her husband's defense. "But she's still living a Plan B life. If you are not married and raising children, it's Plan B."

Still wincing at the pain I knew some of those young adults experienced, several days later I still wished I'd had the good sense to say at the time that which I had thought of overnight: "The truth is that there is only one plan, and that is the Plan of Salvation in which the Lord invites us all to participate."

June, a sensitive and learned friend, tells of the time a well-meaning bishopric member announced to the congregation, "We're happy to tell you that Brother Clint Jones has a new grandchild." June, Brother Jones' second wife, married him twenty years ago after his first wife died. Sitting by him and their own two sons, June thought of her years raising the daughter whose new baby had just been announced to the ward. Ouch!

Sally, a wise woman, sighed when she shared the experience of her son and daughter-in-law. Unable to have a family for many years, they finally adopted. After three months, the young birth mother recanted her promises and took the baby back. The couple was heart broken. Many months later, Sally's daughter-in-law announced at a family birthday party that she was pregnant. Amidst the rejoicing, Sally's sister said loudly to her own children, "Well, now you'll have a real cousin." Such insensitivity is haunting.

We talk much these days of diversity and non-traditional families. That is good, but it seems the kind of dialogue that, out of context, can pull us off the mark. I think the point of all that fine talk is not how much we're different, but rather how much we should be connected.

The truth is that there is only one plan. We are all sons and daughters of God, connected to families—by blood, by adoption, by affection, and by ward affiliation. And we have so much to offer each other.

Jesus said, "I am the way, the truth, and the life: no man cometh unto the Father, but by me" (John 14:6). In a sense, we all stand outside the house of perfection. Very few live up to even a portion of the image of perfection—the perfectly happy couple with their perfect children in the perfect house surrounding the perfect table on which lie the scriptures, perfectly marked. What the Savior teaches is that we don't have to be in that perfect house in order to partake of His perfect truths.

The truth is that our Savior "doeth that which is good among the children of men; and he doeth nothing save it be plain unto the children of men; and he inviteth them all to come unto him and partake of his goodness; and he denieth none that come unto him, black and white, bond and free, male and female; and he remembereth the heathen; and all are alike unto God, both Jew and Gentile" (2 Nephi 26:33).

That's the truth that I pray those young Relief Society leaders will espouse, whenever they marry.

U is for Unity

I was sometimes an unsympathetic older sister. I was the kind who painted my eight and nine year-old brothers' fingernails red after they'd gone to sleep. I hope they've forgiven me—especially for laughing so hard the morning after.

Despite all such adolescent romping, my parents worked very hard to help us feel unity in our family. They tolerated and even valued much of the sibling give-and-take in our home, but I always knew they wanted us to join together as a strong unit.

They made unending attempts at family home evening, never with more than moderate success. Neither lavish desserts, nor promises of Saturday motorcycle rides, nor parental cajoling, nor sibling taunting, nor any teaching approach ever got one of my brothers off the floor and into a chair, Book of Mormon in hand.

My parents, like so many parents, worked incessantly to put us in situations where unity could occur. Mom and Dad took us on weekly pilgrimages to see grandparents. They insisted we participate in family reunions. They scheduled extended family parties at our home, summer after summer.

I recall lots of hesitant family prayers and reluctant work parties. I also remember the hilarious family vacations, the silly made-up jokes, the popcorn on Sunday nights, the retellings of triumph on the golf course or romance at the junior prom. Ours were never the home evenings featured in Church magazines nor were our family parties the stuff of magazine articles, but in a thousand warm, funny, poignant, daily ways, our parents generated an environment in which unity could grow.

Now that we're all adults, we still work on unity. We have had to re-create some of our relationships. With each marriage and baby, we build something more and, hopefully, better. We help each other move in and out of state. We bring bottles of soup to the sick among us. We counsel about new Church callings and changes in occupation. We run up long distance phone bills telling stories of minor glories and pains. We don't always respond as sensitively as we might.

We honor our beloved mother who gets most of the credit for the unity we experienced as children at home. We still eat popcorn together on Sunday nights, and we teach a new generation to be unified.

So it is in families who hold unity as a supreme goal.

One of my earliest memorable lessons in family unity came when I was fourteen. I was very angry with my darling sister Alice for some long-forgotten reason. In the heat of the anger, I called a friend and lambasted my sister. When I hung up, my father took me aside privately and clearly explained that if I were upset, I needed to talk directly with Alice. Under no circumstances should I criticize her outside the family. Our family needed to be unified, my father said, and in order to do that we owed each other loyalty.

On one occasion when I had felt particularly injured by some thoughtless behavior by a co-worker, I told my mother about the situation. She rallied to my aid. She called my sister, who dropped everything and immediately called me. Mom also called Stan, my brother, who put aside what he was doing and called. Mom and Alice took me to lunch, loved me up, and reassured me. Stan drove ninety miles just to bring me some flowers and a card. All that care took place within twenty-four hours of the incident.

That show of loyalty and love was so healing that it deep cleaned what could have been a long-lasting injury. Family unity, built of many years of interaction, began to heal me almost before I had time to hurt.

Wilford Woodruff taught:

> "If we will unite in one, acting in good faith, every man esteeming his brother as himself, regarding not what he possesses as his own, but the Lord's, all carrying out these principles, the result is certain—it is the enjoyment of the Spirit of the Lord, it is the light of eternity, it is the abundance of all things of this earth; it is an opportunity to provide education for our children, amusement and interest for ourselves, a knowledge of the things of the kingdom of God, and all sciences which are embraced therein, and an advance in the work of the last days, preparatory to the redemption of the centre stake of Zion" (Journal of Discourses, vol. 17, p. 73).

My own life experience validates that although family life will not always be easy and although we live in homes that may be far from perfect, the unity that parents can build into a family does indeed bring enjoyment, knowledge, light and surety.

V IS FOR VALIANT

Valiant people are clear, as pure water is clear. The valiant person's life echoes Shakespeare's words, "I love the name of honor more than I fear death."

"Trustworthy," "loyal," "straight," and "honorable" are words well applied to people who prove themselves valiant in supporting the gospel of Jesus Christ. Their behavior refreshes the spirit, as clear water refreshes the body.

One of my favorite scriptural images is that found in James. "But be ye doers of the word, and not hearers only, deceiving your own selves.

"For if any be a hearer of the word, and not a doer, he is like unto a man beholding his natural face in a glass:

> For he beholdeth himself, and goeth his way, and straightway forgetteth what manner of man he was (James 1:22-24).

James' message here is more than "just do it." I think James wants us both to do and to understand that doers of the word see themselves in a spiritual mirror, not just a physical one. Indeed, for the valiant, what we see is what we get, for valiant behavior is a show of internal characteristics, just as a mirror is a reflection of who looks into it.

On my last birthday, I returned home to my condo to find that my small garden in the back was filled with favorite flowers. Geraniums and columbines joined other varieties in gorgeous array not only in my backyard but also in my front garden patch. When I saw this beautiful gift, I wept. I knew who had planted these wonders, a woman in my ward with whom I served in an auxiliary. Weeks before at a meeting we had talked gardens, and I had said something about wanting flowers but not knowing what to plant in my small, shady spaces.

Without a word, the right flowers appeared. Nothing she could have done or said spoke more of love than the gift she chose. Her actions also bespoke that she was valiant in acting upon what she professed to believe. I learned a great lesson from this thoughtful pledge of friendship given by a woman who is as clearly valiant as refreshing water.

While Joseph Smith was in Liberty Jail, he pled with the Lord for the Saints who were suffering greatly. The Lord's answer, of which the following is part, fills the soul:

> For there is a time appointed for every man, according as his works shall be.
> God shall give you knowledge by his Holy Spirit, yea, by the unspeakable gift of the Holy Ghost, that has not been revealed since the world was until now;
> Which our forefathers have awaited with anxious expectation to be revealed in the last times, which their minds were pointed to by the angels, as held in reserve for the fullness of their glory;
> A time to come in the which nothing shall be with-

held, whether there be one God or many gods, they shall be manifest.

All thrones and dominions, principalities and powers, shall be revealed and set forth upon all who have endured valiantly for the gospel of Jesus Christ (D&C 121:25-29).

So here we are, in the fullness of times, when "nothing shall be withheld;" in fact, all "shall be revealed and set forth" upon the valiant.

The prophets have usually used the word "valiant" in talking about heroic soldiers. People, like my horticulturally gifted friend, are valiant too. They do well what they can where they are, and what better can anyone do?

A few verses later in D&C 121, the question is asked, "How long can rolling waters remain impure?" (D&C 121:33). For the valiant, those who act on what they believe, the answer is, "Not long." My observation has been that valiant people often run over some rocks, yet they hurry on, anxious to get about the Lord's work.

Those obstacles polish rough edges as they purify. Rolling waters and valiant people press forward in all weather, over all obstacles. Thus the valiant, like pure water, become clear. Thus, the trustworthy, honorable, valiant souls of the earth refresh us.

W IS FOR WHAT MATTERS

What matters? From our life experiences we learn new answers to that question all the time. But we will never find a more significant one than "faith." Faith is what matters.

I believe that one of the best parts of maturing is the realization that the real things always matter, they just matter in different ways as we age. Sometimes when we are inexperienced or confused, we temporarily forget what matters. Faith, like many things, may be put aside momentarily or remain undiscovered through decades. Although the Lord's goodness to us is evidenced everyday in the rising of the sun, the glory of the flowers, the warmth of the sun, and thousands of other ways, faith in Him can rest in someone's heart, untried and untapped for years. Faith often surfaces eventually, as life experiences call our attention to how reliant we always are on the Lord, while so much else in our lives comes and goes.

As styles come, then recycle a generation later, so opportunities to develop faith come and come around again. The banality of some of our concerns need not permanently banish faith. In fact, our passing concerns may serve as the counterpoint that makes faith more real.

The following commentary, of sorts, identifies some ways I've thought about what matters most as we grow up and, hopefully, grow in faith.

In A Word

WHAT MATTERS

When You're 20	When You're 30	When You're 40+
1. The color of your date's hair	His occupation	His character
2. Being liked	Being a key player	Being respected
3. Staying up all night worrying about	Staying up all night talking to friends	Staying up all caring for children
4. A car of your own	A hot car of your own	A car of your own
5. Having adventures	Being able to afford adventures	Maintaining sufficient energy during the adventures
6. Seeking fun	Seeking friends	Seeking meaning
7. Picnics with your date	Time to have picnics with your family	Clean, safe places to have picnics and time with your family
8. Having to read so much for college classes	Having to read so much for work	Not having enough time to read
9. Learning how to work	Learning how to work harder	Learning how to work smarter
10. Making a good salary	Making a better salary	Making enough salary to retire on
11. How much it costs to get your hair done	Finding time to get your hair done	Paying any cost to find enough hair to get done

12. The ideals of the system	The machinations of the system	How to restore the ideals to the machinations of the system
13. Owning your own home	Redoing your own home	Keeping up your own home
14. Eating new foods	Eating stylish foods	Taking off the weight from all the new and stylish foods you ate at 20 and 30
15. Faith	Faith	Faith

Despite all the ebb and flow of daily life, despite all the foibles and fun of being younger or older, what matters most is faith.

The first Article of Faith begins, "We believe. . ." That's what faith is about: believing. The fourth Article explains that the "first principles and ordinances of the Gospel are: first, Faith in the Lord Jesus Christ. . . ."

We start with faith. Our beliefs, as members of The Church of Jesus Christ of Latter-day Saints begin with our faith, that is, "our confidence in something or someone" (*Bible Dictionary*, p. 669). Without faith, the "substance of things hoped for, the evidence of things not seen," we cannot please our Lord (Hebrews 11:1, 6).

For some of us, that knowledge came in our twenties or even younger. For some of us, the reality of faith distilled upon us in later decades. Faith endures, no matter what our age or interests or concerns. We begin and endure through faith.

Faith matters—it matters most.

X IS FOR X'D

Sometimes I dream that on one of the many forms I seem to fill out each year, I'll encounter a section in which I can "x" that which marks the spot. There is food that hits the spot, but I'm not talking about anything so fleeting. I would like to place my vote by those actions and attitudes that are "spot on." I'd love to encounter a "check all that apply" list on which I can put my "x" by attitudes, ideas, and life approaches that make life more wonderful.

These are some of what I want to "x":

1. The Big Four: Please, Thank You, Excuse Me, I'm Sorry.

I'd like to have the Big Four made part of every school curricula and every driver's education class, every Scout program and every Young Women class. Basic courtesy is much underestimated and much needed.

2. Functional families.

Thank you for making your family functional. On behalf of all of us who work/deal/share roads with your children, thank you for all you taught them.

Thank you for saying "No" when it was needed.

Thank you for teaching the hard lessons, including, "Wait your turn in line." "Hold your temper." "Pick up after yourself." "Burping in public is not polite." "We don't use that word." "We won't watch that program in our home." "Watch where you walk, dear, so you don't step on the nice lady."

Thank you for letting your children be children in childhood so they may be adults, rather than adolescents, in future times.

Thank you for letting them deal with rebellion and responsibility in turn, so when they work with me, they function like decent human beings.

Thank you for loving them and loving them and loving them. Because of what you did then, your children are fine people now. I am grateful for your functional family.

3. Minds well used.
   The Lord put brains, not meatballs, in our heads for a reason.

4. The dictionary.
   One way to overcome the world is to rise above its exceedingly limited vocabulary.

5. Scriptures everywhere.

Keep a small one in the glove compartment to fill the minutes while we wait for traffic lights or children after school. A large one by the kitchen sink to read while we do the dishes. A compact one in our fishing vests to refresh our spirits and give the fish a rest. Scriptures by our bed, scripture tapes in the players we take on morning walks, scripture CDs on our computers.

Let's inundate ourselves and our families with the scriptures, the ultimate surround sound for the soul.

6. Fullness of life in the fullness of times.

Imagine how blessed we are—living when new temples spring up annually, having the means to serve, owning machines that make life easier, knowing all that the Lord has ever revealed is here upon the earth at this time. I say, let's make our lives full of the fullness that is ours in this, the fullness of times.

7. Mortality in all its confusion.

William Wordsworth said we come to mortality "trailing clouds of glory."

James Thurber said we go through life "trailing a glory of cloudiness."

I say, "Enjoy the clouds and stay on the trail."

8. Personal progress.

My Annual Test of Personal Progress

   a. Did I send the first Christmas card of the season to the person who gave me the hardest time during the year?

   b. Was I long-suffering with the grocery store clerks?

   c. Did I play with the children?

   d. Did I rejoice in truth whenever I read it, heard, saw it, lived it?

Y IS FOR YEA

I love the word "yea." It means an affirmative statement or vote. For lots of people it also means a cheer. I like both meanings.

The Lord said, "But let your communication be, Yea, yea; Nay, nay: for whatsoever is more than these cometh of evil" (Matt. 5:37). "Yea" is obviously a powerful word, for it represents our affirmation and commitment. James said it this way, "But above all things, my brethren, swear not, neither by heaven, neither by the earth, neither by any other oath: but let your yea be yea; and your nay, nay; lest ye fall under condemnation" (James 5:12).

Obviously, the Lord does not want us to swear, but I think the message is also that we should mean something by our yeas. When we put our arms to the square in church and acknowledge each other's callings, that's a form of saying "Yea." It's a commitment to performance, not simply a comment that's perfunctory.

In my early twenties I had my first dip into the real world of Church service when I was called as a ward homemaking counselor in a singles ward Relief Society presidency. I remember well the day the bishop asked me to arrange for a meal after church on the days we had firesides. With no thought I responded, "Why? That will be a lot of work for the presidency, and everyone can just eat at home."

Showing a lot of charity, the bishop kindly explained the need to me. Many ward members, he reminded me, lived a long way from the meetinghouse. If the Relief Society didn't prepare a meal, they'd have to bring a lunch or buy one or go hungry since most of them stayed at the chapel until the fireside. We had inadequate facilities to refrigerate lunches, we didn't want the Saints to violate the Sabbath by buying food, and we didn't want people to go hungry. So, as the homemaking counselor, it fell to me to arrange for lunches.

Of course it was my job, but I was so inexperienced all I could see was my own inconvenience. The needs of those I was called to serve had not crossed my mind. I did not yet understand that when I had said, "Yea" in answer to the call, I had committed myself to that sort of service.

With the help of more seasoned ward members, I set up the meals, and I began to look at and after others. In my young life this was a great moment and great fun. I am sure that without the mutual commitment and hoagie sandwiches we shared, members of that presidency and I would not keep in touch as we still do.

Saying yea to the right things brings rich rewards. "Yea, I will do it" is a green light. It opens the way and gets things moving. Paul understood this principle. He wrote to the saints in Corinth, "...do I purpose according to the flesh, that with me there should be yea yea, and nay nay?

"But as God is true, our word toward you was not yea and nay.

"For the Son of God, Jesus Christ, who was preached among you by us, even by me and Silvanus and

Timotheus, was not yea and nay, but in him was yea.

"For all the promises of God in him are yea, and in him Amen, unto the glory of God by us" (2 Corinthians 1:17-20). Paul was not ambivalent; he was committed, and yea represented that for him. With Paul, yea meant yea.

So it was with John the Revelator. He wrote, "I know thy works, that thou art neither cold nor hot: I would thou wert cold or hot" (Revelation 3:15). Indeed, yea should mean yea.

And that is the point and why I love the word "yea." It's a short word that is long on meaning. It represents commitment and purpose and service.

For all who say yea and mean it, I cheer, "Yea!"

Z IS FOR ZEAL

Zeal is not bravado.

It is consistent best effort.

It is not bombast.

Zeal is enthusiastic adherence to the gospel.

John the Revelator taught, "Be zealous, therefore, and repent" (Rev. 3:19). Alma admonished us to be "zealous for keeping the commandments of God" (Alma 21:23). These prophets seem to be saying, "Once more with feeling now."

Sometimes zeal gets a bad rap because zealots, even those engaged in good causes, can go overboard. But the type of zeal that moves us toward repentance and obedience is much to be desired.

When we feel zeal for a cause, we can do great things. Zeal well channeled is behind every successful stake service project and beautiful ward choir. Behind every successful High Priest party, Relief Society retreat and youth fireside are people with sufficient zeal to pull events together and to pull them off.

I think of a time when I was serving in an auxiliary. We were holding a first fireside of the new year. Somehow signals got crossed and none of us had made proper arrangements to set up the refreshments. There we sat on the stand with no unobtrusive way to get to the cultural hall where the refreshments sat on the lip of the stage.

As the meeting progressed, I got more and more nervous. I kept thinking about those trays of food and sacks of cups and the people who would rush to enjoy them as soon as the meeting ended. I felt quite helpless until I noticed some movement on a back bench. Two brethren, one the husband of a ward auxiliary leader, looked at the clock and whispered to each other. Then they quietly made their way out of the chapel.

By the time I got into the cultural hall, after wending my way down a very crowded aisle, the refreshments were laid out on two tables. The zeal of these two good men rescued us.

In some cases, zeal can cover a multitude of errors and absences. Even if we don't know everything, even when we don't have everything, we can do what we do know with what we have in a zealous spirit of enthusiastic devotion.

I had occasion once to talk with a woman who was the Relief Society president of a small branch of the church in Eastern Europe. The Saints were spread over many miles, resources were scarce and leadership almost non-existent. The sisters who could convene on Sunday met in this woman's kitchen. They had two manuals, both in English, so the Relief Society president, the only one who read English well, taught every week. Visiting teaching was virtually impossible, for the women lacked money, telephones, and time. This president remained undaunted. She understood the problems, but she did not see them as being insurmountable.

She and the other sisters who could meet would write monthly cards to the sisters far away. Whenever someone traveled to another area of the ward, they penned a note to the sisters in that area so a visit might be arranged. When the English manual discussed things these women didn't have, like freezers, the Relief Society president adapted the materials.

What inspired me was how "ho-hum" she was about these challenges and how zealous she was about solutions. The facts of her life did not smother her zeal; in fact, they seemed to fan her desire to serve. I believe that without this president's zeal, the entire branch Relief Society would have disappeared.

I don't think that zeal is the gift of only the young and strong or the mature and wise. Zeal can appear in great bursts of energy, on the frontiers of faith, and in moments of grand drama. It is equally prevalent in the quiet corners of today's existence, behind the step-by-step plodding that life often requires. Modern and historic pioneers have put one foot in front of the other, and kept moving on. That's zeal too. Sometimes just living peacefully with a lot of issues beyond our control requires an extraordinary show of zeal for the good cause.

Zeal is not a flash in the pan.

It is not noisy or noisome.

Zeal is happy, heroic, consistent.

It is a get-up-and-do-it manner of living.

That's why it can move us to higher ground and motivate us to be our best selves and to do our best work.

About the Author

Carol L. Clark earned a Ph.D. from the University of Utah. She has held positions in education and government and is currently Manager of Training in the LDS Church's Family and Church History Department. She served on the Relief Society General Board under three presidents.

9 26575 76402 7